MATH
SPEED DRILLS

- ☑ **ADDITION**
- ☑ **SUBTRACTION**
- ☑ **MULTIPLICATION**
- ☑ **LONG DIVISION**
- ☑ **FRACTIONS**
- ☑ **DECIMALS**

GRADE 5

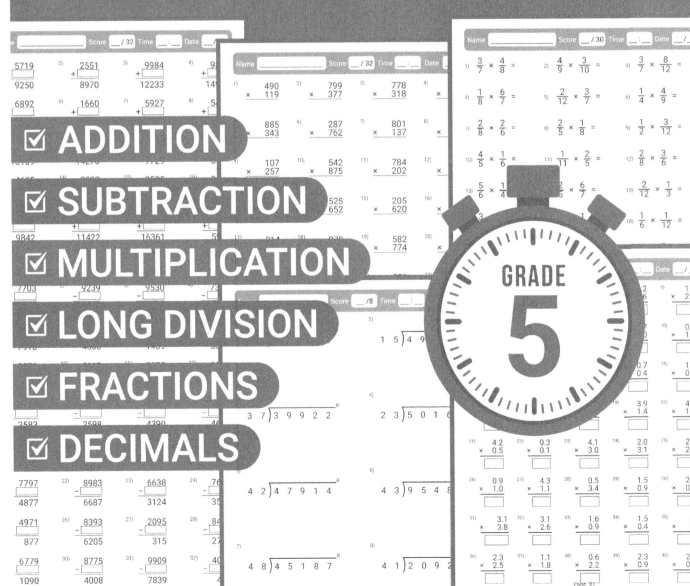

This Workbook Belongs to:

_____

Table of Contents

Other math workbooks for your gifted 5th grader...

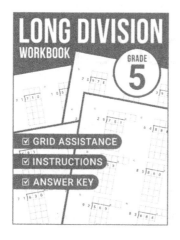

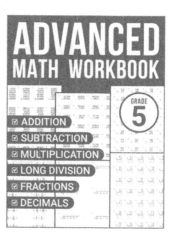

Scan the QR code below:

Scan the QR code below:

Scan the QR code below:

Scan the QR code below:

www.Nermilio.com

Level 1

Addition

Adding 4-digit numbers
(missing addends)

1) 5719
  + [   ]
    9250

2) 2551
  + [   ]
    8970

3) 9984
  + [   ]
    12233

4) 9855
  + [   ]
    14995

5) 6892
  + [   ]
    16374

6) 1660
  + [   ]
    10829

7) 5927
  + [   ]
    9636

8) 5420
  + [   ]
    14997

9) 9932
  + [   ]
    18109

10) 6737
   + [   ]
     14270

11) 5869
   + [   ]
     7729

12) 3424
   + [   ]
     5786

13) 4605
   + [   ]
     12039

14) 2992
   + [   ]
     5610

15) 9585
   + [   ]
     11826

16) 9671
   + [   ]
     17680

17) 7990
   + [   ]
     9842

18) 2762
   + [   ]
     11422

19) 8551
   + [   ]
     16361

20) 2811
   + [   ]
     5970

21) 3175
   + [   ]
     5753

22) 1903
   + [   ]
     4092

23) 4780
   + [   ]
     14112

24) 9226
   + [   ]
     11658

25) 2373
   + [   ]
     7520

26) 3291
   + [   ]
     9699

27) 8393
   + [   ]
     14613

28) 6500
   + [   ]
     15310

29) 9278
   + [   ]
     13804

30) 1163
   + [   ]
     4402

31) 6671
   + [   ]
     12073

32) 7718
   + [   ]
     11091

1) 3088
+ [____]
10386

2) 4795
+ [____]
12535

3) 1247
+ [____]
7893

4) 1867
+ [____]
7419

5) 7361
+ [____]
14480

6) 7469
+ [____]
16829

7) 2469
+ [____]
12382

8) 2079
+ [____]
9004

9) 2457
+ [____]
6191

10) 9709
+ [____]
16634

11) 8261
+ [____]
9924

12) 2066
+ [____]
7508

13) 7933
+ [____]
16658

14) 4172
+ [____]
12985

15) 9311
+ [____]
14851

16) 3830
+ [____]
12690

17) 3196
+ [____]
9512

18) 7389
+ [____]
14388

19) 2102
+ [____]
6165

20) 6447
+ [____]
14078

21) 5165
+ [____]
14264

22) 2462
+ [____]
10394

23) 6509
+ [____]
10602

24) 8927
+ [____]
10447

25) 6495
+ [____]
12643

26) 8192
+ [____]
13995

27) 3463
+ [____]
9454

28) 9841
+ [____]
12876

29) 5456
+ [____]
6807

30) 7480
+ [____]
15716

31) 4611
+ [____]
13223

32) 5995
+ [____]
8548

1) 5942
   + [   ]
    7839

2) 2966
   + [   ]
    9720

3) 4967
   + [   ]
    13030

4) 6002
   + [   ]
    10512

5) 2702
   + [   ]
    10059

6) 4610
   + [   ]
    14318

7) 4584
   + [   ]
    8647

8) 6707
   + [   ]
    12561

9) 6611
   + [   ]
    12388

10) 1751
   + [   ]
    10900

11) 3292
   + [   ]
    8097

12) 9253
   + [   ]
    12401

13) 4859
   + [   ]
    13202

14) 6336
   + [   ]
    12356

15) 4054
   + [   ]
    13032

16) 9169
   + [   ]
    15931

17) 1632
   + [   ]
    3082

18) 5839
   + [   ]
    13358

19) 9603
   + [   ]
    18979

20) 2082
   + [   ]
    9554

21) 7393
   + [   ]
    15951

22) 3821
   + [   ]
    11114

23) 5423
   + [   ]
    7478

24) 4331
   + [   ]
    14053

25) 3126
   + [   ]
    10362

26) 5338
   + [   ]
    10358

27) 5031
   + [   ]
    11172

28) 6839
   + [   ]
    13544

29) 4082
   + [   ]
    8021

30) 1848
   + [   ]
    5112

31) 7450
   + [   ]
    17374

32) 5530
   + [   ]
    7614

1) 3047
   + [____]
    4448

2) 9469
   + [____]
    15581

3) 4902
   + [____]
    11368

4) 2613
   + [____]
    12329

5) 4813
   + [____]
    11783

6) 6124
   + [____]
    8079

7) 2349
   + [____]
    3466

8) 8962
   + [____]
    11190

9) 6508
   + [____]
    11157

10) 8385
   + [____]
    13305

11) 9145
   + [____]
    17218

12) 7628
   + [____]
    10719

13) 3934
   + [____]
    7833

14) 6364
   + [____]
    8358

15) 9688
   + [____]
    13074

16) 5799
   + [____]
    12410

17) 7553
   + [____]
    11164

18) 8139
   + [____]
    11636

19) 6536
   + [____]
    13157

20) 9827
   + [____]
    15900

21) 7763
   + [____]
    16348

22) 6224
   + [____]
    14207

23) 3092
   + [____]
    5209

24) 2297
   + [____]
    4799

25) 9486
   + [____]
    17658

26) 4075
   + [____]
    12837

27) 7782
   + [____]
    10005

28) 6656
   + [____]
    7833

29) 2134
   + [____]
    11733

30) 4178
   + [____]
    11465

31) 9710
   + [____]
    17740

32) 2993
   + [____]
    8173

1) 4469
   + [ ]
   8970

2) 6819
   + [ ]
   15550

3) 3513
   + [ ]
   9463

4) 7425
   + [ ]
   14276

5) 2037
   + [ ]
   9199

6) 1809
   + [ ]
   8209

7) 8944
   + [ ]
   16000

8) 5713
   + [ ]
   15038

9) 3043
   + [ ]
   4172

10) 3260
    + [ ]
    4801

11) 7174
    + [ ]
    8325

12) 9032
    + [ ]
    16767

13) 1084
    + [ ]
    10556

14) 8015
    + [ ]
    9371

15) 8864
    + [ ]
    11776

16) 7596
    + [ ]
    17071

17) 9971
    + [ ]
    17124

18) 9265
    + [ ]
    19070

19) 8823
    + [ ]
    17713

20) 1792
    + [ ]
    11219

21) 9120
    + [ ]
    17949

22) 9037
    + [ ]
    15138

23) 4461
    + [ ]
    9309

24) 9717
    + [ ]
    18534

25) 6112
    + [ ]
    15803

26) 4299
    + [ ]
    7702

27) 9829
    + [ ]
    18628

28) 6714
    + [ ]
    14920

29) 8982
    + [ ]
    10715

30) 3638
    + [ ]
    8158

31) 9719
    + [ ]
    17858

32) 3367
    + [ ]
    9933

1) 4971
  + [____]
   12219

2) 9972
  + [____]
   11694

3) 3498
  + [____]
   9253

4) 1555
  + [____]
   8765

5) 1329
  + [____]
   4445

6) 3152
  + [____]
   10359

7) 8441
  + [____]
   9976

8) 1771
  + [____]
   3342

9) 5046
  + [____]
   12055

10) 8017
  + [____]
   12354

11) 6396
  + [____]
   15808

12) 8071
  + [____]
   13955

13) 4685
  + [____]
   11698

14) 9676
  + [____]
   17961

15) 9506
  + [____]
   16039

16) 3840
  + [____]
   7678

17) 8519
  + [____]
   10567

18) 1820
  + [____]
   10177

19) 6887
  + [____]
   13708

20) 2151
  + [____]
   4154

21) 9589
  + [____]
   16764

22) 6377
  + [____]
   12904

23) 2724
  + [____]
   9880

24) 4620
  + [____]
   13332

25) 3414
  + [____]
   5034

26) 1211
  + [____]
   5695

27) 2131
  + [____]
   12119

28) 4066
  + [____]
   5094

29) 3901
  + [____]
   5421

30) 7477
  + [____]
   17042

31) 2523
  + [____]
   5458

32) 3825
  + [____]
   11757

1) 7364 + ☐ = 10759

2) 9953 + ☐ = 12942

3) 8313 + ☐ = 10782

4) 1432 + ☐ = 7630

5) 6713 + ☐ = 16500

6) 9977 + ☐ = 16136

7) 9332 + ☐ = 17962

8) 3343 + ☐ = 12287

9) 9167 + ☐ = 16951

10) 4678 + ☐ = 10523

11) 3260 + ☐ = 4390

12) 8470 + ☐ = 16831

13) 7456 + ☐ = 15725

14) 1672 + ☐ = 7677

15) 2908 + ☐ = 4235

16) 8962 + ☐ = 18021

17) 5593 + ☐ = 6995

18) 5249 + ☐ = 7563

19) 6527 + ☐ = 10780

20) 9583 + ☐ = 11269

21) 7819 + ☐ = 15320

22) 1631 + ☐ = 6005

23) 4527 + ☐ = 13820

24) 1274 + ☐ = 6225

25) 4609 + ☐ = 7419

26) 5323 + ☐ = 12445

27) 7323 + ☐ = 11304

28) 5650 + ☐ = 13290

29) 1208 + ☐ = 10042

30) 4615 + ☐ = 11976

31) 5210 + ☐ = 9319

32) 6246 + ☐ = 10075

Level 2

Subtraction

Subtracting 4-digit numbers
(missing subtrahend)

1) 7703
  − [ ]
  ─────
    403

2) 9239
  − [ ]
  ─────
   3483

3) 9530
  − [ ]
  ─────
   6697

4) 7325
  − [ ]
  ─────
   1364

5) 9738
  − [ ]
  ─────
   7916

6) 6213
  − [ ]
  ─────
   4666

7) 4161
  − [ ]
  ─────
   1409

8) 5392
  − [ ]
  ─────
   3044

9) 5570
  − [ ]
  ─────
   3523

10) 5887
   − [ ]
   ─────
     567

11) 7075
   − [ ]
   ─────
    3552

12) 9841
   − [ ]
   ─────
    3141

13) 8958
   − [ ]
   ─────
    2583

14) 5314
   − [ ]
   ─────
    2598

15) 7458
   − [ ]
   ─────
    4390

16) 5965
   − [ ]
   ─────
    4623

17) 4351
   − [ ]
   ─────
    1387

18) 4259
   − [ ]
   ─────
     801

19) 6238
   − [ ]
   ─────
    4955

20) 4312
   − [ ]
   ─────
    2436

21) 7797
   − [ ]
   ─────
    4877

22) 8983
   − [ ]
   ─────
    6687

23) 6638
   − [ ]
   ─────
    3124

24) 7687
   − [ ]
   ─────
    3594

25) 4971
   − [ ]
   ─────
     877

26) 8393
   − [ ]
   ─────
    6205

27) 2095
   − [ ]
   ─────
     315

28) 8482
   − [ ]
   ─────
    2775

29) 6779
   − [ ]
   ─────
    1090

30) 8775
   − [ ]
   ─────
    4008

31) 9909
   − [ ]
   ─────
    7839

32) 4023
   − [ ]
   ─────
     471

1) 5703 − [ ] = 2890

2) 4972 − [ ] = 3399

3) 9074 − [ ] = 2685

4) 9560 − [ ] = 2700

5) 2718 − [ ] = 54

6) 5043 − [ ] = 217

7) 8462 − [ ] = 4862

8) 5450 − [ ] = 1143

9) 2889 − [ ] = 1018

10) 8777 − [ ] = 4807

11) 8586 − [ ] = 2743

12) 5056 − [ ] = 2349

13) 8431 − [ ] = 5249

14) 9169 − [ ] = 842

15) 9642 − [ ] = 566

16) 7700 − [ ] = 3498

17) 7611 − [ ] = 969

18) 7248 − [ ] = 2261

19) 7886 − [ ] = 6634

20) 7413 − [ ] = 2762

21) 7840 − [ ] = 2053

22) 9239 − [ ] = 2659

23) 9515 − [ ] = 2858

24) 9615 − [ ] = 2418

25) 6882 − [ ] = 5750

26) 7947 − [ ] = 6505

27) 9069 − [ ] = 5320

28) 9021 − [ ] = 5457

29) 8467 − [ ] = 4136

30) 8758 − [ ] = 3065

31) 8943 − [ ] = 7761

32) 6947 − [ ] = 3074

1)
```
  6248
-  [    ]
  2135
```

2)
```
  5610
-  [    ]
   559
```

3)
```
  8430
-  [    ]
  6730
```

4)
```
  4747
-  [    ]
  2189
```

5)
```
  7801
-  [    ]
   890
```

6)
```
  4929
-  [    ]
  3793
```

7)
```
  8929
-  [    ]
  1354
```

8)
```
  5726
-  [    ]
  1875
```

9)
```
  3983
-  [    ]
  2075
```

10)
```
  4263
-  [    ]
  2164
```

11)
```
  8404
-  [    ]
  6830
```

12)
```
  7674
-  [    ]
  5913
```

13)
```
  7937
-  [    ]
  2746
```

14)
```
  9990
-  [    ]
  4386
```

15)
```
  2807
-  [    ]
  1150
```

16)
```
  6728
-  [    ]
  1368
```

17)
```
  8999
-  [    ]
  6457
```

18)
```
  7105
-  [    ]
  4375
```

19)
```
  9768
-  [    ]
  1213
```

20)
```
  3384
-  [    ]
  2323
```

21)
```
  4288
-  [    ]
  1975
```

22)
```
  9681
-  [    ]
  4829
```

23)
```
  7842
-  [    ]
  2315
```

24)
```
  5497
-  [    ]
   526
```

25)
```
  4246
-  [    ]
  2127
```

26)
```
  5774
-  [    ]
  2199
```

27)
```
  6427
-  [    ]
  2361
```

28)
```
  9088
-  [    ]
   633
```

29)
```
  3659
-  [    ]
  1939
```

30)
```
  8254
-  [    ]
  5918
```

31)
```
  6078
-  [    ]
    56
```

32)
```
  5481
-  [    ]
  4219
```

1) 9055 − ☐ = 7426

2) 4310 − ☐ = 758

3) 2859 − ☐ = 784

4) 9798 − ☐ = 5969

5) 3081 − ☐ = 978

6) 9203 − ☐ = 5548

7) 4521 − ☐ = 1336

8) 9992 − ☐ = 951

9) 4674 − ☐ = 3173

10) 6689 − ☐ = 1776

11) 8781 − ☐ = 2376

12) 9356 − ☐ = 2074

13) 5322 − ☐ = 770

14) 6816 − ☐ = 2042

15) 9609 − ☐ = 7246

16) 7384 − ☐ = 851

17) 7945 − ☐ = 2193

18) 6004 − ☐ = 3817

19) 5921 − ☐ = 4277

20) 7827 − ☐ = 4018

21) 6729 − ☐ = 2157

22) 5193 − ☐ = 3976

23) 7509 − ☐ = 5641

24) 9157 − ☐ = 5292

25) 9706 − ☐ = 5839

26) 7665 − ☐ = 3194

27) 7479 − ☐ = 1117

28) 5644 − ☐ = 868

29) 9870 − ☐ = 8488

30) 7694 − ☐ = 3644

31) 5740 − ☐ = 4582

32) 1726 − ☐ = 665

1) 4729
  − [   ]
    1454

2) 9482
  − [   ]
    792

3) 5589
  − [   ]
    2486

4) 6054
  − [   ]
    995

5) 9336
  − [   ]
    3325

6) 9385
  − [   ]
    5121

7) 7969
  − [   ]
    665

8) 8176
  − [   ]
    6132

9) 6330
  − [   ]
    4314

10) 8186
   − [   ]
     1923

11) 2058
   − [   ]
     83

12) 4705
   − [   ]
     3195

13) 7394
   − [   ]
     3555

14) 4389
   − [   ]
     1647

15) 4218
   − [   ]
     2972

16) 4885
   − [   ]
     2585

17) 3291
   − [   ]
     249

18) 9751
   − [   ]
     6085

19) 4452
   − [   ]
     255

20) 5927
   − [   ]
     2162

21) 4407
   − [   ]
     2417

22) 7162
   − [   ]
     3330

23) 7667
   − [   ]
     5891

24) 8280
   − [   ]
     1449

25) 5928
   − [   ]
     4236

26) 7117
   − [   ]
     5697

27) 8178
   − [   ]
     3815

28) 4079
   − [   ]
     480

29) 7290
   − [   ]
     44

30) 6955
   − [   ]
     739

31) 7310
   − [   ]
     6300

32) 4743
   − [   ]
     1219

1) 5437 − ☐ = 1835

2) 5287 − ☐ = 876

3) 9598 − ☐ = 3470

4) 7342 − ☐ = 1855

5) 9236 − ☐ = 7761

6) 5165 − ☐ = 2095

7) 4924 − ☐ = 1278

8) 6255 − ☐ = 896

9) 3583 − ☐ = 857

10) 3841 − ☐ = 192

11) 2680 − ☐ = 1008

12) 9063 − ☐ = 7656

13) 5106 − ☐ = 2071

14) 7646 − ☐ = 3772

15) 9103 − ☐ = 7767

16) 6926 − ☐ = 3856

17) 6376 − ☐ = 925

18) 6195 − ☐ = 1904

19) 9648 − ☐ = 5802

20) 6512 − ☐ = 1555

21) 9603 − ☐ = 8463

22) 5947 − ☐ = 3543

23) 9014 − ☐ = 4778

24) 8780 − ☐ = 1081

25) 4016 − ☐ = 2949

26) 5755 − ☐ = 1647

27) 7533 − ☐ = 3810

28) 7457 − ☐ = 5306

29) 7114 − ☐ = 3294

30) 8313 − ☐ = 3771

31) 7044 − ☐ = 555

32) 6146 − ☐ = 218

1)
```
  5676
-[    ]
------
  1321
```

2)
```
  8370
-[    ]
------
  4663
```

3)
```
  6245
-[    ]
------
  4814
```

4)
```
  9637
-[    ]
------
  4450
```

5)
```
  9490
-[    ]
------
  2638
```

6)
```
  6926
-[    ]
------
  2768
```

7)
```
  2687
-[    ]
------
   255
```

8)
```
  9983
-[    ]
------
  8473
```

9)
```
  9095
-[    ]
------
  7776
```

10)
```
  7547
-[    ]
------
  1592
```

11)
```
  4067
-[    ]
------
  1364
```

12)
```
  8582
-[    ]
------
  5286
```

13)
```
  8654
-[    ]
------
  5985
```

14)
```
  5278
-[    ]
------
   845
```

15)
```
  7765
-[    ]
------
  5186
```

16)
```
  9794
-[    ]
------
  6668
```

17)
```
  9390
-[    ]
------
  7200
```

18)
```
  5145
-[    ]
------
  1194
```

19)
```
  3639
-[    ]
------
  1634
```

20)
```
  9413
-[    ]
------
  7379
```

21)
```
  6994
-[    ]
------
  5920
```

22)
```
  5315
-[    ]
------
  3552
```

23)
```
  6849
-[    ]
------
   837
```

24)
```
  7913
-[    ]
------
  6027
```

25)
```
  4622
-[    ]
------
  1570
```

26)
```
  9575
-[    ]
------
  3344
```

27)
```
  5409
-[    ]
------
  3148
```

28)
```
  5698
-[    ]
------
  2040
```

29)
```
  9037
-[    ]
------
  7891
```

30)
```
  7641
-[    ]
------
  5673
```

31)
```
  4461
-[    ]
------
   939
```

32)
```
  8242
-[    ]
------
   156
```

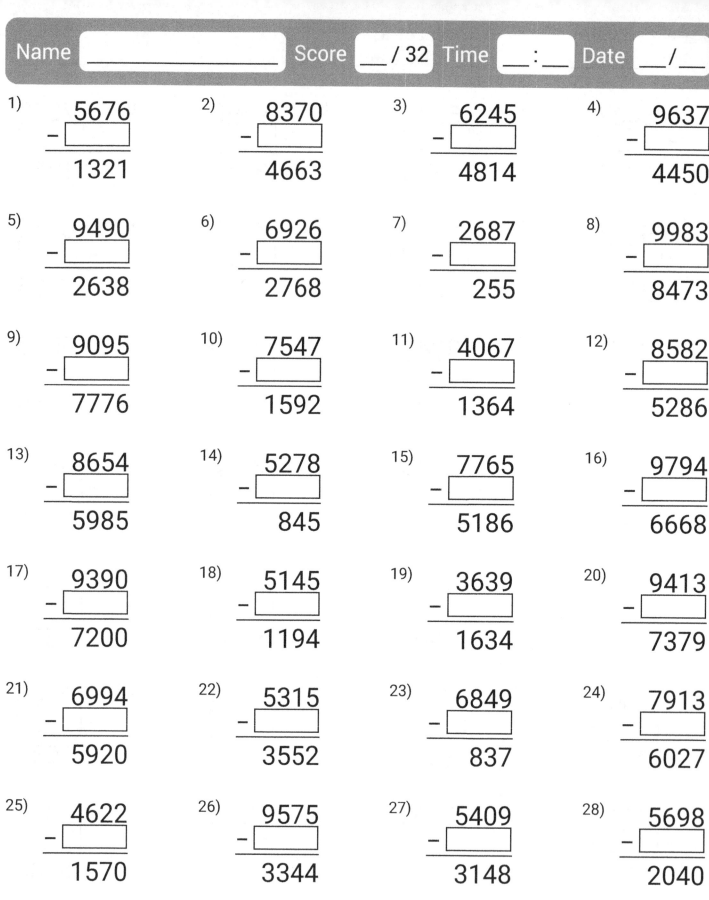

Level 3

Multiplication

Multiplying 3-digit by 3-digit numbers

1) 490
  × 119

2) 799
  × 377

3) 778
  × 318

4) 926
  × 659

5) 885
  × 343

6) 287
  × 762

7) 801
  × 137

8) 446
  × 743

9) 107
  × 257

10) 542
  × 875

11) 784
  × 202

12) 703
  × 809

13) 930
  × 816

14) 525
  × 652

15) 205
  × 620

16) 189
  × 566

17) 214
  × 141

18) 978
  × 579

19) 582
  × 774

20) 459
  × 287

21) 874
  × 474

22) 101
  × 570

23) 559
  × 894

24) 994
  × 787

25) 909
  × 121

26) 776
  × 632

27) 724
  × 106

28) 131
  × 972

29) 961
  × 151

30) 204
  × 194

31) 384
  × 450

32) 338
  × 905

1)
$$810 \times 220$$

2)
$$240 \times 174$$

3)
$$535 \times 342$$

4)
$$355 \times 971$$

5)
$$304 \times 436$$

6)
$$953 \times 102$$

7)
$$741 \times 441$$

8)
$$857 \times 879$$

9)
$$922 \times 359$$

10)
$$736 \times 684$$

11)
$$485 \times 775$$

12)
$$619 \times 333$$

13)
$$809 \times 408$$

14)
$$723 \times 373$$

15)
$$820 \times 874$$

16)
$$480 \times 698$$

17)
$$749 \times 422$$

18)
$$906 \times 500$$

19)
$$304 \times 929$$

20)
$$483 \times 877$$

21)
$$712 \times 650$$

22)
$$618 \times 239$$

23)
$$142 \times 107$$

24)
$$735 \times 420$$

25)
$$326 \times 881$$

26)
$$879 \times 214$$

27)
$$493 \times 919$$

28)
$$485 \times 490$$

29)
$$300 \times 623$$

30)
$$244 \times 981$$

31)
$$695 \times 411$$

32)
$$738 \times 998$$

1)
```
    645
×   349
```

2)
```
    668
×   175
```

3)
```
    888
×   332
```

4)
```
    336
×   287
```

5)
```
    627
×   346
```

6)
```
    978
×   576
```

7)
```
    630
×   810
```

8)
```
    231
×   487
```

9)
```
    924
×   458
```

10)
```
    595
×   668
```

11)
```
    704
×   988
```

12)
```
    432
×   661
```

13)
```
    608
×   719
```

14)
```
    831
×   237
```

15)
```
    813
×   875
```

16)
```
    880
×   576
```

17)
```
    398
×   683
```

18)
```
    752
×   268
```

19)
```
    363
×   683
```

20)
```
    972
×   489
```

21)
```
    988
×   875
```

22)
```
    545
×   152
```

23)
```
    228
×   479
```

24)
```
    187
×   326
```

25)
```
    139
×   668
```

26)
```
    805
×   490
```

27)
```
    767
×   795
```

28)
```
    205
×   588
```

29)
```
    825
×   437
```

30)
```
    152
×   806
```

31)
```
    246
×   951
```

32)
```
    538
×   720
```

1)
$$\begin{array}{r} 793 \\ \times\ 435 \\ \hline \end{array}$$

2)
$$\begin{array}{r} 873 \\ \times\ 875 \\ \hline \end{array}$$

3)
$$\begin{array}{r} 969 \\ \times\ 160 \\ \hline \end{array}$$

4)
$$\begin{array}{r} 233 \\ \times\ 269 \\ \hline \end{array}$$

5)
$$\begin{array}{r} 759 \\ \times\ 120 \\ \hline \end{array}$$

6)
$$\begin{array}{r} 181 \\ \times\ 256 \\ \hline \end{array}$$

7)
$$\begin{array}{r} 559 \\ \times\ 500 \\ \hline \end{array}$$

8)
$$\begin{array}{r} 899 \\ \times\ 937 \\ \hline \end{array}$$

9)
$$\begin{array}{r} 395 \\ \times\ 813 \\ \hline \end{array}$$

10)
$$\begin{array}{r} 164 \\ \times\ 880 \\ \hline \end{array}$$

11)
$$\begin{array}{r} 741 \\ \times\ 615 \\ \hline \end{array}$$

12)
$$\begin{array}{r} 536 \\ \times\ 190 \\ \hline \end{array}$$

13)
$$\begin{array}{r} 427 \\ \times\ 667 \\ \hline \end{array}$$

14)
$$\begin{array}{r} 735 \\ \times\ 181 \\ \hline \end{array}$$

15)
$$\begin{array}{r} 476 \\ \times\ 292 \\ \hline \end{array}$$

16)
$$\begin{array}{r} 255 \\ \times\ 664 \\ \hline \end{array}$$

17)
$$\begin{array}{r} 424 \\ \times\ 823 \\ \hline \end{array}$$

18)
$$\begin{array}{r} 505 \\ \times\ 340 \\ \hline \end{array}$$

19)
$$\begin{array}{r} 167 \\ \times\ 470 \\ \hline \end{array}$$

20)
$$\begin{array}{r} 568 \\ \times\ 668 \\ \hline \end{array}$$

21)
$$\begin{array}{r} 150 \\ \times\ 826 \\ \hline \end{array}$$

22)
$$\begin{array}{r} 188 \\ \times\ 549 \\ \hline \end{array}$$

23)
$$\begin{array}{r} 642 \\ \times\ 955 \\ \hline \end{array}$$

24)
$$\begin{array}{r} 524 \\ \times\ 849 \\ \hline \end{array}$$

25)
$$\begin{array}{r} 392 \\ \times\ 757 \\ \hline \end{array}$$

26)
$$\begin{array}{r} 535 \\ \times\ 599 \\ \hline \end{array}$$

27)
$$\begin{array}{r} 952 \\ \times\ 270 \\ \hline \end{array}$$

28)
$$\begin{array}{r} 896 \\ \times\ 723 \\ \hline \end{array}$$

29)
$$\begin{array}{r} 234 \\ \times\ 375 \\ \hline \end{array}$$

30)
$$\begin{array}{r} 234 \\ \times\ 462 \\ \hline \end{array}$$

31)
$$\begin{array}{r} 226 \\ \times\ 364 \\ \hline \end{array}$$

32)
$$\begin{array}{r} 203 \\ \times\ 152 \\ \hline \end{array}$$

1)
```
    873
×   978
```

2)
```
    162
×   795
```

3)
```
    245
×   253
```

4)
```
    483
×   761
```

5)
```
    177
×   739
```

6)
```
    737
×   984
```

7)
```
    427
×   413
```

8)
```
    511
×   265
```

9)
```
    499
×   540
```

10)
```
    418
×   828
```

11)
```
    631
×   841
```

12)
```
    228
×   120
```

13)
```
    284
×   348
```

14)
```
    292
×   966
```

15)
```
    263
×   789
```

16)
```
    540
×   238
```

17)
```
    934
×   448
```

18)
```
    890
×   898
```

19)
```
    228
×   736
```

20)
```
    183
×   169
```

21)
```
    983
×   887
```

22)
```
    130
×   603
```

23)
```
    422
×   532
```

24)
```
    760
×   191
```

25)
```
    938
×   879
```

26)
```
    906
×   994
```

27)
```
    303
×   667
```

28)
```
    719
×   105
```

29)
```
    201
×   713
```

30)
```
    696
×   767
```

31)
```
    177
×   821
```

32)
```
    212
×   636
```

1)
```
    534
  ×  407
```

2)
```
    160
  ×  950
```

3)
```
    585
  ×  117
```

4)
```
    764
  ×  401
```

5)
```
    532
  ×  203
```

6)
```
    801
  ×  245
```

7)
```
    731
  ×  945
```

8)
```
    331
  ×  342
```

9)
```
    306
  ×  959
```

10)
```
    993
  ×  730
```

11)
```
    454
  ×  303
```

12)
```
    439
  ×  894
```

13)
```
    853
  ×  862
```

14)
```
    597
  ×  765
```

15)
```
    258
  ×  321
```

16)
```
    561
  ×  716
```

17)
```
    440
  ×  219
```

18)
```
    699
  ×  585
```

19)
```
    524
  ×  914
```

20)
```
    544
  ×  844
```

21)
```
    539
  ×  709
```

22)
```
    163
  ×  793
```

23)
```
    917
  ×  684
```

24)
```
    287
  ×  151
```

25)
```
    262
  ×  723
```

26)
```
    977
  ×  315
```

27)
```
    404
  ×  946
```

28)
```
    552
  ×  682
```

29)
```
    477
  ×  687
```

30)
```
    921
  ×  484
```

31)
```
    155
  ×  608
```

32)
```
    536
  ×  898
```

1)
$$\begin{array}{r} 508 \\ \times\ 193 \\ \hline \end{array}$$

2)
$$\begin{array}{r} 885 \\ \times\ 219 \\ \hline \end{array}$$

3)
$$\begin{array}{r} 101 \\ \times\ 625 \\ \hline \end{array}$$

4)
$$\begin{array}{r} 639 \\ \times\ 784 \\ \hline \end{array}$$

5)
$$\begin{array}{r} 895 \\ \times\ 685 \\ \hline \end{array}$$

6)
$$\begin{array}{r} 351 \\ \times\ 232 \\ \hline \end{array}$$

7)
$$\begin{array}{r} 923 \\ \times\ 339 \\ \hline \end{array}$$

8)
$$\begin{array}{r} 583 \\ \times\ 747 \\ \hline \end{array}$$

9)
$$\begin{array}{r} 772 \\ \times\ 425 \\ \hline \end{array}$$

10)
$$\begin{array}{r} 833 \\ \times\ 482 \\ \hline \end{array}$$

11)
$$\begin{array}{r} 589 \\ \times\ 202 \\ \hline \end{array}$$

12)
$$\begin{array}{r} 723 \\ \times\ 355 \\ \hline \end{array}$$

13)
$$\begin{array}{r} 963 \\ \times\ 883 \\ \hline \end{array}$$

14)
$$\begin{array}{r} 535 \\ \times\ 541 \\ \hline \end{array}$$

15)
$$\begin{array}{r} 585 \\ \times\ 854 \\ \hline \end{array}$$

16)
$$\begin{array}{r} 720 \\ \times\ 550 \\ \hline \end{array}$$

17)
$$\begin{array}{r} 705 \\ \times\ 490 \\ \hline \end{array}$$

18)
$$\begin{array}{r} 457 \\ \times\ 729 \\ \hline \end{array}$$

19)
$$\begin{array}{r} 332 \\ \times\ 292 \\ \hline \end{array}$$

20)
$$\begin{array}{r} 835 \\ \times\ 325 \\ \hline \end{array}$$

21)
$$\begin{array}{r} 116 \\ \times\ 449 \\ \hline \end{array}$$

22)
$$\begin{array}{r} 292 \\ \times\ 131 \\ \hline \end{array}$$

23)
$$\begin{array}{r} 852 \\ \times\ 249 \\ \hline \end{array}$$

24)
$$\begin{array}{r} 409 \\ \times\ 127 \\ \hline \end{array}$$

25)
$$\begin{array}{r} 577 \\ \times\ 305 \\ \hline \end{array}$$

26)
$$\begin{array}{r} 807 \\ \times\ 248 \\ \hline \end{array}$$

27)
$$\begin{array}{r} 107 \\ \times\ 715 \\ \hline \end{array}$$

28)
$$\begin{array}{r} 174 \\ \times\ 906 \\ \hline \end{array}$$

29)
$$\begin{array}{r} 638 \\ \times\ 161 \\ \hline \end{array}$$

30)
$$\begin{array}{r} 985 \\ \times\ 821 \\ \hline \end{array}$$

31)
$$\begin{array}{r} 858 \\ \times\ 917 \\ \hline \end{array}$$

32)
$$\begin{array}{r} 237 \\ \times\ 342 \\ \hline \end{array}$$

Level 4

Division

Long division with remainders
(divisors 10-50)

1)

$$20 \overline{)24782} ^R$$

2)

$$15 \overline{)49838} ^R$$

3)

$$37 \overline{)39922} ^R$$

4)

$$23 \overline{)50161} ^R$$

5)

$$42 \overline{)47914} ^R$$

6)

$$43 \overline{)95484} ^R$$

7)

$$48 \overline{)45187} ^R$$

8)

$$41 \overline{)20923} ^R$$

1)

$$19 \overline{)4\ 2\ 6\ 1\ 8}\ ^R$$

2)

$$14 \overline{)4\ 9\ 6\ 4\ 5}\ ^R$$

3)

$$24 \overline{)1\ 2\ 9\ 0\ 0}\ ^R$$

4)

$$15 \overline{)8\ 4\ 3\ 8\ 7}\ ^R$$

5)

$$41 \overline{)7\ 9\ 0\ 4\ 5}\ ^R$$

6)

$$19 \overline{)3\ 8\ 0\ 3\ 5}\ ^R$$

7)

$$34 \overline{)2\ 7\ 0\ 6\ 5}\ ^R$$

8)

$$42 \overline{)7\ 5\ 1\ 4\ 6}\ ^R$$

1)

$$33\overline{)76811}\,^R$$

2)

$$42\overline{)84825}\,^R$$

3)

$$24\overline{)48606}\,^R$$

4)

$$46\overline{)61662}\,^R$$

5)

$$46\overline{)58702}\,^R$$

6)

$$18\overline{)77931}\,^R$$

7)

$$43\overline{)29089}\,^R$$

8)

$$26\overline{)20444}\,^R$$

1)

$$40 \overline{)903711} \,^R$$

2)

$$48 \overline{)564452} \,^R$$

3)

$$23 \overline{)531154} \,^R$$

4)

$$29 \overline{)181866} \,^R$$

5)

$$28 \overline{)840092} \,^R$$

6)

$$30 \overline{)376977} \,^R$$

7)

$$29 \overline{)196511} \,^R$$

8)

$$13 \overline{)101955} \,^R$$

1)

$$24\overline{)79243}\,^R$$

2)

$$39\overline{)84604}\,^R$$

3)

$$45\overline{)99814}\,^R$$

4)

$$32\overline{)64814}\,^R$$

5)

$$26\overline{)18115}\,^R$$

6)

$$35\overline{)27942}\,^R$$

7)

$$22\overline{)75372}\,^R$$

8)

$$15\overline{)12404}\,^R$$

1)
```
     _____R
4 7 ) 4 1 2 1 4
```

2)
```
     _____R
4 1 ) 1 8 7 7 1
```

3)
```
     _____R
1 4 ) 9 2 4 9 6
```

4)
```
     _____R
4 5 ) 2 5 9 4 4
```

5)
```
     _____R
2 4 ) 4 8 7 0 8
```

6)
```
     _____R
4 3 ) 2 9 4 1 8
```

7)
```
     _____R
3 6 ) 1 1 5 5 7
```

8)
```
     _____R
1 9 ) 1 0 5 4 1
```

Level 5

Fractions

Adding mixed numbers with unlike denominators

1) $2\frac{6}{17} + 3\frac{5}{11} =$

2) $7\frac{3}{6} + 1\frac{16}{25} =$

3) $1\frac{13}{35} + 1\frac{6}{24} =$

4) $1\frac{4}{41} + 1\frac{1}{49} =$

5) $1\frac{16}{25} + 1\frac{1}{38} =$

6) $1\frac{11}{33} + 1\frac{4}{41} =$

7) $1\frac{11}{37} + 1\frac{11}{38} =$

8) $2\frac{2}{13} + 1\frac{19}{25} =$

9) $1\frac{19}{20} + 1\frac{8}{22} =$

10) $9\frac{1}{4} + 1\frac{19}{23} =$

11) $2\frac{2}{21} + 1\frac{1}{46} =$

12) $1\frac{6}{43} + 1\frac{12}{35} =$

13) $1\frac{12}{22} + 2\frac{10}{18} =$

14) $1\frac{17}{28} + 1\frac{6}{34} =$

15) $1\frac{7}{43} + 2\frac{5}{17} =$

16) $1\frac{12}{32} + 1\frac{4}{44} =$

17) $1\frac{3}{43} + 1\frac{6}{39} =$

18) $1\frac{8}{12} + 1\frac{5}{14} =$

19) $2\frac{2}{23} + 1\frac{11}{36} =$

20) $1\frac{1}{34} + 3\frac{5}{15} =$

1) $3\frac{7}{13} + 2\frac{8}{21} =$

2) $2\frac{2}{12} + 1\frac{20}{29} =$

3) $1\frac{10}{37} + 2\frac{1}{21} =$

4) $1\frac{16}{21} + 1\frac{9}{34} =$

5) $2\frac{5}{16} + 1\frac{8}{25} =$

6) $3\frac{11}{13} + 1\frac{19}{31} =$

7) $1\frac{4}{41} + 2\frac{6}{21} =$

8) $1\frac{4}{33} + 1\frac{10}{39} =$

9) $1\frac{14}{25} + 1\frac{1}{11} =$

10) $1\frac{1}{49} + 1\frac{6}{32} =$

11) $2\frac{8}{19} + 1\frac{1}{48} =$

12) $1\frac{10}{28} + 2\frac{3}{19} =$

13) $1\frac{5}{39} + 1\frac{7}{36} =$

14) $1\frac{10}{36} + 1\frac{19}{25} =$

15) $2\frac{2}{8} + 1\frac{11}{19} =$

16) $1\frac{17}{23} + 1\frac{5}{13} =$

17) $9\frac{1}{5} + 1\frac{4}{45} =$

18) $1\frac{6}{41} + 1\frac{1}{45} =$

19) $2\frac{2}{13} + 1\frac{3}{40} =$

20) $1\frac{2}{38} + 1\frac{14}{17} =$

1) $1\frac{10}{26} + 1\frac{2}{38} =$

2) $1\frac{8}{12} + 1\frac{12}{33} =$

3) $6\frac{1}{2} + 1\frac{16}{33} =$

4) $1\frac{11}{28} + 1\frac{1}{25} =$

5) $1\frac{4}{16} + 1\frac{2}{38} =$

6) $1\frac{6}{42} + 1\frac{12}{13} =$

7) $1\frac{5}{30} + 1\frac{1}{49} =$

8) $3\frac{7}{10} + 1\frac{7}{42} =$

9) $1\frac{13}{37} + 1\frac{5}{45} =$

10) $1\frac{4}{37} + 1\frac{4}{38} =$

11) $1\frac{14}{34} + 1\frac{5}{14} =$

12) $1\frac{11}{26} + 1\frac{10}{22} =$

13) $1\frac{12}{15} + 1\frac{20}{29} =$

14) $1\frac{1}{30} + 1\frac{6}{37} =$

15) $4\frac{7}{8} + 1\frac{2}{41} =$

16) $1\frac{3}{25} + 1\frac{3}{29} =$

17) $1\frac{5}{43} + 1\frac{16}{19} =$

18) $1\frac{6}{41} + 2\frac{4}{17} =$

19) $1\frac{2}{22} + 2\frac{2}{19} =$

20) $2\frac{6}{15} + 1\frac{22}{25} =$

1) $1\frac{12}{28} + 1\frac{2}{46} =$

2) $1\frac{3}{14} + 1\frac{19}{20} =$

3) $1\frac{2}{42} + 1\frac{3}{40} =$

4) $1\frac{2}{43} + 1\frac{11}{27} =$

5) $1\frac{1}{49} + 1\frac{19}{31} =$

6) $1\frac{3}{39} + 1\frac{2}{14} =$

7) $3\frac{3}{9} + 1\frac{2}{48} =$

8) $1\frac{6}{7} + 1\frac{2}{37} =$

9) $1\frac{9}{26} + 1\frac{3}{41} =$

10) $1\frac{6}{29} + 1\frac{24}{25} =$

11) $1\frac{3}{36} + 1\frac{15}{27} =$

12) $1\frac{1}{38} + 1\frac{15}{25} =$

13) $1\frac{5}{36} + 1\frac{5}{32} =$

14) $1\frac{6}{40} + 1\frac{17}{33} =$

15) $1\frac{7}{25} + 1\frac{12}{36} =$

16) $1\frac{12}{16} + 2\frac{2}{22} =$

17) $1\frac{22}{26} + 1\frac{21}{27} =$

18) $1\frac{6}{14} + 1\frac{2}{43} =$

19) $1\frac{14}{30} + 1\frac{9}{11} =$

20) $1\frac{18}{27} + 1\frac{7}{36} =$

1) $1\frac{2}{46} + 1\frac{5}{31} =$

2) $2\frac{5}{21} + 1\frac{8}{37} =$

3) $1\frac{4}{45} + 1\frac{8}{37} =$

4) $1\frac{16}{23} + 3\frac{5}{10} =$

5) $1\frac{6}{12} + 1\frac{15}{31} =$

6) $1\frac{2}{4} + 1\frac{6}{43} =$

7) $1\frac{8}{25} + 1\frac{3}{30} =$

8) $3\frac{1}{8} + 2\frac{1}{13} =$

9) $1\frac{7}{30} + 3\frac{4}{13} =$

10) $8\frac{1}{5} + 1\frac{8}{29} =$

11) $1\frac{1}{46} + 1\frac{10}{20} =$

12) $1\frac{21}{24} + 1\frac{13}{27} =$

13) $1\frac{6}{33} + 1\frac{1}{28} =$

14) $1\frac{2}{32} + 1\frac{2}{48} =$

15) $1\frac{3}{25} + 1\frac{11}{35} =$

16) $9\frac{3}{5} + 1\frac{1}{41} =$

17) $1\frac{16}{17} + 1\frac{12}{38} =$

18) $1\frac{11}{33} + 1\frac{7}{19} =$

19) $1\frac{3}{41} + 1\frac{9}{37} =$

20) $5\frac{4}{9} + 4\frac{5}{11} =$

1) $1\dfrac{1}{37} + 2\dfrac{7}{18} =$

2) $1\dfrac{14}{24} + 3\dfrac{10}{13} =$

3) $11\dfrac{2}{3} + 1\dfrac{2}{31} =$

4) $1\dfrac{9}{41} + 1\dfrac{15}{28} =$

5) $1\dfrac{2}{42} + 1\dfrac{2}{21} =$

6) $1\dfrac{12}{33} + 1\dfrac{4}{35} =$

7) $1\dfrac{1}{30} + 1\dfrac{4}{40} =$

8) $1\dfrac{9}{36} + 1\dfrac{3}{29} =$

9) $1\dfrac{12}{23} + 1\dfrac{10}{35} =$

10) $1\dfrac{6}{42} + 1\dfrac{3}{35} =$

11) $1\dfrac{6}{19} + 1\dfrac{3}{45} =$

12) $2\dfrac{4}{16} + 3\dfrac{6}{13} =$

13) $1\dfrac{8}{24} + 1\dfrac{12}{16} =$

14) $1\dfrac{11}{32} + 1\dfrac{4}{14} =$

15) $1\dfrac{5}{45} + 1\dfrac{12}{30} =$

16) $2\dfrac{2}{13} + 1\dfrac{1}{36} =$

17) $2\dfrac{7}{19} + 3\dfrac{2}{16} =$

18) $5\dfrac{4}{5} + 2\dfrac{11}{12} =$

19) $3\dfrac{8}{14} + 1\dfrac{5}{17} =$

20) $5\dfrac{2}{8} + 1\dfrac{11}{27} =$

Level 6

Fractions

Subtracting mixed numbers with unlike denominators

1) $4\frac{2}{11} - 1\frac{6}{21} =$

2) $10\frac{2}{4} - 1\frac{7}{35} =$

3) $1\frac{12}{18} - 1\frac{8}{39} =$

4) $11\frac{2}{4} - 1\frac{20}{26} =$

5) $1\frac{9}{29} - 1\frac{6}{41} =$

6) $1\frac{15}{20} - 1\frac{8}{33} =$

7) $5\frac{6}{8} - 1\frac{7}{26} =$

8) $1\frac{6}{34} - 1\frac{3}{27} =$

9) $1\frac{9}{37} - 1\frac{3}{44} =$

10) $2\frac{10}{15} - 2\frac{4}{11} =$

11) $1\frac{9}{35} - 1\frac{6}{32} =$

12) $1\frac{10}{26} - 1\frac{11}{31} =$

13) $1\frac{5}{44} - 1\frac{1}{43} =$

14) $1\frac{2}{7} - 1\frac{1}{26} =$

15) $1\frac{7}{42} - 1\frac{1}{23} =$

16) $1\frac{7}{35} - 1\frac{5}{38} =$

17) $1\frac{4}{15} - 1\frac{1}{45} =$

18) $2\frac{11}{17} - 1\frac{13}{32} =$

19) $2\frac{11}{19} - 1\frac{3}{45} =$

20) $3\frac{4}{13} - 1\frac{10}{38} =$

1) $2\frac{1}{12} - 1\frac{9}{35} =$

2) $1\frac{19}{28} - 1\frac{14}{27} =$

3) $1\frac{5}{13} - 1\frac{6}{40} =$

4) $1\frac{18}{32} - 1\frac{13}{37} =$

5) $9\frac{4}{5} - 1\frac{4}{39} =$

6) $1\frac{20}{23} - 1\frac{3}{36} =$

7) $2\frac{13}{17} - 1\frac{11}{29} =$

8) $2\frac{11}{19} - 1\frac{11}{39} =$

9) $1\frac{22}{24} - 1\frac{10}{34} =$

10) $5\frac{7}{8} - 1\frac{1}{20} =$

11) $1\frac{16}{32} - 1\frac{3}{42} =$

12) $5\frac{1}{2} - 1\frac{1}{49} =$

13) $1\frac{12}{35} - 1\frac{2}{47} =$

14) $1\frac{13}{21} - 1\frac{3}{25} =$

15) $3\frac{2}{15} - 1\frac{7}{37} =$

16) $1\frac{7}{21} - 1\frac{8}{42} =$

17) $1\frac{5}{36} - 1\frac{2}{34} =$

18) $3\frac{4}{14} - 1\frac{14}{17} =$

19) $1\frac{12}{37} - 1\frac{3}{38} =$

20) $3\frac{2}{15} - 1\frac{3}{23} =$

1) $1\frac{24}{25} - 1\frac{19}{31} =$

2) $1\frac{2}{45} - 1\frac{1}{37} =$

3) $2\frac{5}{10} - 1\frac{7}{21} =$

4) $2\frac{3}{10} - 1\frac{14}{19} =$

5) $3\frac{11}{12} - 1\frac{3}{39} =$

6) $1\frac{12}{34} - 1\frac{1}{46} =$

7) $1\frac{17}{33} - 1\frac{13}{27} =$

8) $3\frac{8}{14} - 1\frac{12}{33} =$

9) $1\frac{7}{40} - 1\frac{2}{47} =$

10) $1\frac{20}{22} - 1\frac{15}{23} =$

11) $1\frac{6}{29} - 1\frac{1}{49} =$

12) $1\frac{12}{36} - 1\frac{8}{39} =$

13) $1\frac{12}{27} - 1\frac{8}{36} =$

14) $1\frac{9}{28} - 1\frac{1}{39} =$

15) $5\frac{2}{4} - 1\frac{8}{30} =$

16) $8\frac{1}{6} - 4\frac{4}{10} =$

17) $2\frac{5}{11} - 1\frac{12}{16} =$

18) $2\frac{1}{23} - 1\frac{19}{31} =$

19) $2\frac{2}{20} - 1\frac{1}{11} =$

20) $2\frac{4}{22} - 2\frac{4}{23} =$

1) $3\frac{3}{12} - 1\frac{4}{38} =$

2) $1\frac{11}{34} - 1\frac{3}{42} =$

3) $3\frac{3}{11} - 1\frac{2}{27} =$

4) $4\frac{1}{11} - 2\frac{7}{20} =$

5) $3\frac{6}{12} - 1\frac{5}{19} =$

6) $1\frac{2}{44} - 1\frac{2}{48} =$

7) $2\frac{8}{15} - 1\frac{7}{40} =$

8) $2\frac{2}{10} - 1\frac{12}{36} =$

9) $1\frac{7}{38} - 1\frac{7}{42} =$

10) $1\frac{13}{29} - 1\frac{2}{18} =$

11) $5\frac{4}{5} - 1\frac{1}{44} =$

12) $5\frac{1}{2} - 1\frac{18}{29} =$

13) $1\frac{1}{44} - 1\frac{1}{49} =$

14) $5\frac{6}{8} - 1\frac{4}{17} =$

15) $1\frac{19}{22} - 1\frac{5}{29} =$

16) $1\frac{10}{27} - 1\frac{7}{43} =$

17) $1\frac{15}{28} - 1\frac{2}{39} =$

18) $2\frac{1}{18} - 1\frac{6}{42} =$

19) $1\frac{18}{28} - 1\frac{2}{44} =$

20) $3\frac{2}{4} - 2\frac{6}{14} =$

1) $1\frac{13}{14} - 1\frac{1}{24} =$

2) $2\frac{6}{13} - 1\frac{1}{44} =$

3) $5\frac{1}{3} - 1\frac{16}{23} =$

4) $1\frac{19}{23} - 1\frac{2}{45} =$

5) $1\frac{12}{23} - 1\frac{9}{38} =$

6) $1\frac{7}{23} - 1\frac{3}{47} =$

7) $2\frac{6}{11} - 2\frac{1}{19} =$

8) $1\frac{7}{9} - 1\frac{4}{44} =$

9) $1\frac{5}{31} - 1\frac{5}{38} =$

10) $1\frac{5}{13} - 1\frac{11}{30} =$

11) $3\frac{7}{12} - 1\frac{1}{49} =$

12) $2\frac{6}{16} - 1\frac{3}{39} =$

13) $1\frac{14}{32} - 1\frac{1}{47} =$

14) $2\frac{5}{22} - 1\frac{6}{32} =$

15) $1\frac{10}{20} - 1\frac{7}{30} =$

16) $1\frac{10}{18} - 1\frac{5}{45} =$

17) $1\frac{11}{19} - 1\frac{6}{42} =$

18) $2\frac{6}{11} - 1\frac{1}{23} =$

19) $1\frac{6}{15} - 1\frac{10}{32} =$

20) $4\frac{2}{6} - 3\frac{2}{16} =$

1) $1\frac{10}{20} - 1\frac{1}{43} =$

2) $4\frac{1}{7} - 1\frac{3}{32} =$

3) $1\frac{5}{40} - 1\frac{2}{45} =$

4) $1\frac{17}{27} - 1\frac{2}{22} =$

5) $5\frac{2}{7} - 1\frac{11}{39} =$

6) $4\frac{3}{6} - 2\frac{2}{15} =$

7) $2\frac{5}{8} - 2\frac{3}{11} =$

8) $1\frac{8}{40} - 1\frac{5}{34} =$

9) $1\frac{18}{26} - 1\frac{12}{38} =$

10) $2\frac{3}{17} - 1\frac{7}{27} =$

11) $1\frac{13}{30} - 1\frac{1}{42} =$

12) $1\frac{6}{44} - 1\frac{1}{23} =$

13) $1\frac{13}{19} - 1\frac{1}{17} =$

14) $4\frac{2}{10} - 1\frac{8}{38} =$

15) $1\frac{22}{28} - 1\frac{2}{47} =$

16) $1\frac{3}{27} - 1\frac{2}{48} =$

17) $11\frac{2}{4} - 1\frac{1}{26} =$

18) $24\frac{1}{2} - 1\frac{10}{38} =$

19) $2\frac{1}{14} - 1\frac{5}{36} =$

20) $2\frac{8}{10} - 1\frac{11}{18} =$

Level 7

Fractions

Multiplying fractions
(denominators 2-12)

1) $\dfrac{3}{7} \times \dfrac{4}{8} =$

2) $\dfrac{4}{9} \times \dfrac{3}{10} =$

3) $\dfrac{3}{7} \times \dfrac{8}{12} =$

4) $\dfrac{1}{8} \times \dfrac{6}{7} =$

5) $\dfrac{2}{12} \times \dfrac{3}{7} =$

6) $\dfrac{1}{4} \times \dfrac{4}{9} =$

7) $\dfrac{2}{8} \times \dfrac{2}{6} =$

8) $\dfrac{2}{5} \times \dfrac{1}{8} =$

9) $\dfrac{1}{2} \times \dfrac{3}{12} =$

10) $\dfrac{4}{5} \times \dfrac{1}{6} =$

11) $\dfrac{1}{11} \times \dfrac{2}{5} =$

12) $\dfrac{2}{8} \times \dfrac{3}{6} =$

13) $\dfrac{5}{6} \times \dfrac{1}{4} =$

14) $\dfrac{2}{5} \times \dfrac{6}{7} =$

15) $\dfrac{2}{12} \times \dfrac{1}{3} =$

16) $\dfrac{3}{4} \times \dfrac{3}{6} =$

17) $\dfrac{2}{4} \times \dfrac{1}{2} =$

18) $\dfrac{1}{6} \times \dfrac{1}{12} =$

19) $\dfrac{5}{6} \times \dfrac{3}{4} =$

20) $\dfrac{1}{2} \times \dfrac{3}{9} =$

21) $\dfrac{6}{8} \times \dfrac{2}{9} =$

22) $\dfrac{3}{4} \times \dfrac{1}{5} =$

23) $\dfrac{2}{4} \times \dfrac{1}{2} =$

24) $\dfrac{2}{5} \times \dfrac{5}{12} =$

25) $\dfrac{10}{12} \times \dfrac{1}{10} =$

26) $\dfrac{4}{8} \times \dfrac{3}{5} =$

27) $\dfrac{3}{8} \times \dfrac{6}{11} =$

28) $\dfrac{1}{8} \times \dfrac{3}{10} =$

29) $\dfrac{2}{3} \times \dfrac{3}{10} =$

30) $\dfrac{2}{8} \times \dfrac{2}{7} =$

1) $\dfrac{2}{8} \times \dfrac{10}{12} =$

2) $\dfrac{7}{12} \times \dfrac{8}{11} =$

3) $\dfrac{4}{6} \times \dfrac{7}{11} =$

4) $\dfrac{7}{9} \times \dfrac{2}{6} =$

5) $\dfrac{2}{3} \times \dfrac{6}{11} =$

6) $\dfrac{10}{12} \times \dfrac{2}{6} =$

7) $\dfrac{8}{9} \times \dfrac{5}{7} =$

8) $\dfrac{2}{9} \times \dfrac{4}{6} =$

9) $\dfrac{1}{5} \times \dfrac{4}{6} =$

10) $\dfrac{4}{5} \times \dfrac{6}{8} =$

11) $\dfrac{1}{3} \times \dfrac{2}{5} =$

12) $\dfrac{1}{2} \times \dfrac{5}{6} =$

13) $\dfrac{3}{6} \times \dfrac{2}{10} =$

14) $\dfrac{1}{8} \times \dfrac{2}{3} =$

15) $\dfrac{3}{7} \times \dfrac{3}{4} =$

16) $\dfrac{1}{2} \times \dfrac{3}{7} =$

17) $\dfrac{3}{4} \times \dfrac{3}{12} =$

18) $\dfrac{5}{7} \times \dfrac{2}{3} =$

19) $\dfrac{1}{2} \times \dfrac{2}{4} =$

20) $\dfrac{1}{4} \times \dfrac{5}{10} =$

21) $\dfrac{4}{12} \times \dfrac{7}{11} =$

22) $\dfrac{2}{7} \times \dfrac{1}{3} =$

23) $\dfrac{4}{6} \times \dfrac{2}{4} =$

24) $\dfrac{9}{11} \times \dfrac{1}{4} =$

25) $\dfrac{9}{10} \times \dfrac{2}{4} =$

26) $\dfrac{5}{11} \times \dfrac{1}{4} =$

27) $\dfrac{1}{3} \times \dfrac{2}{5} =$

28) $\dfrac{1}{9} \times \dfrac{7}{8} =$

29) $\dfrac{1}{2} \times \dfrac{2}{9} =$

30) $\dfrac{5}{8} \times \dfrac{7}{12} =$

1) $\dfrac{3}{8} \times \dfrac{1}{2} =$

2) $\dfrac{8}{11} \times \dfrac{3}{4} =$

3) $\dfrac{2}{3} \times \dfrac{1}{7} =$

4) $\dfrac{8}{11} \times \dfrac{3}{7} =$

5) $\dfrac{6}{12} \times \dfrac{3}{4} =$

6) $\dfrac{1}{2} \times \dfrac{1}{3} =$

7) $\dfrac{6}{8} \times \dfrac{1}{2} =$

8) $\dfrac{5}{7} \times \dfrac{1}{4} =$

9) $\dfrac{1}{5} \times \dfrac{1}{9} =$

10) $\dfrac{2}{5} \times \dfrac{1}{2} =$

11) $\dfrac{2}{5} \times \dfrac{1}{4} =$

12) $\dfrac{5}{7} \times \dfrac{6}{9} =$

13) $\dfrac{2}{5} \times \dfrac{1}{2} =$

14) $\dfrac{2}{4} \times \dfrac{5}{9} =$

15) $\dfrac{3}{8} \times \dfrac{3}{9} =$

16) $\dfrac{3}{6} \times \dfrac{4}{8} =$

17) $\dfrac{3}{10} \times \dfrac{2}{12} =$

18) $\dfrac{8}{10} \times \dfrac{7}{12} =$

19) $\dfrac{7}{8} \times \dfrac{2}{6} =$

20) $\dfrac{3}{4} \times \dfrac{6}{9} =$

21) $\dfrac{1}{8} \times \dfrac{1}{3} =$

22) $\dfrac{8}{12} \times \dfrac{2}{3} =$

23) $\dfrac{1}{6} \times \dfrac{3}{9} =$

24) $\dfrac{1}{2} \times \dfrac{2}{5} =$

25) $\dfrac{2}{3} \times \dfrac{7}{11} =$

26) $\dfrac{2}{7} \times \dfrac{7}{9} =$

27) $\dfrac{6}{7} \times \dfrac{1}{2} =$

28) $\dfrac{2}{4} \times \dfrac{1}{3} =$

29) $\dfrac{1}{10} \times \dfrac{10}{12} =$

30) $\dfrac{8}{10} \times \dfrac{2}{9} =$

1) $\dfrac{1}{2} \times \dfrac{3}{9} =$

2) $\dfrac{3}{5} \times \dfrac{6}{11} =$

3) $\dfrac{1}{2} \times \dfrac{4}{8} =$

4) $\dfrac{6}{9} \times \dfrac{1}{6} =$

5) $\dfrac{7}{11} \times \dfrac{2}{4} =$

6) $\dfrac{2}{9} \times \dfrac{4}{11} =$

7) $\dfrac{1}{10} \times \dfrac{3}{4} =$

8) $\dfrac{5}{11} \times \dfrac{1}{9} =$

9) $\dfrac{9}{10} \times \dfrac{4}{11} =$

10) $\dfrac{4}{10} \times \dfrac{7}{9} =$

11) $\dfrac{1}{2} \times \dfrac{2}{3} =$

12) $\dfrac{2}{11} \times \dfrac{2}{3} =$

13) $\dfrac{2}{3} \times \dfrac{1}{2} =$

14) $\dfrac{4}{5} \times \dfrac{4}{11} =$

15) $\dfrac{1}{3} \times \dfrac{2}{4} =$

16) $\dfrac{2}{5} \times \dfrac{8}{9} =$

17) $\dfrac{1}{4} \times \dfrac{2}{12} =$

18) $\dfrac{1}{2} \times \dfrac{5}{10} =$

19) $\dfrac{1}{3} \times \dfrac{7}{8} =$

20) $\dfrac{2}{3} \times \dfrac{2}{7} =$

21) $\dfrac{2}{3} \times \dfrac{1}{6} =$

22) $\dfrac{2}{5} \times \dfrac{7}{12} =$

23) $\dfrac{2}{8} \times \dfrac{1}{6} =$

24) $\dfrac{2}{11} \times \dfrac{2}{3} =$

25) $\dfrac{1}{4} \times \dfrac{3}{5} =$

26) $\dfrac{2}{8} \times \dfrac{2}{7} =$

27) $\dfrac{3}{4} \times \dfrac{4}{8} =$

28) $\dfrac{4}{5} \times \dfrac{1}{7} =$

29) $\dfrac{1}{8} \times \dfrac{6}{10} =$

30) $\dfrac{2}{10} \times \dfrac{5}{9} =$

1) $\dfrac{1}{6} \times \dfrac{4}{10} =$

2) $\dfrac{2}{3} \times \dfrac{3}{5} =$

3) $\dfrac{2}{10} \times \dfrac{8}{12} =$

4) $\dfrac{2}{8} \times \dfrac{1}{10} =$

5) $\dfrac{3}{4} \times \dfrac{10}{11} =$

6) $\dfrac{7}{8} \times \dfrac{1}{3} =$

7) $\dfrac{1}{10} \times \dfrac{9}{12} =$

8) $\dfrac{2}{9} \times \dfrac{4}{6} =$

9) $\dfrac{2}{3} \times \dfrac{3}{5} =$

10) $\dfrac{2}{6} \times \dfrac{5}{10} =$

11) $\dfrac{3}{10} \times \dfrac{3}{4} =$

12) $\dfrac{4}{12} \times \dfrac{3}{8} =$

13) $\dfrac{2}{12} \times \dfrac{8}{11} =$

14) $\dfrac{8}{10} \times \dfrac{3}{8} =$

15) $\dfrac{1}{4} \times \dfrac{1}{11} =$

16) $\dfrac{7}{9} \times \dfrac{2}{3} =$

17) $\dfrac{1}{2} \times \dfrac{1}{10} =$

18) $\dfrac{10}{12} \times \dfrac{1}{5} =$

19) $\dfrac{5}{7} \times \dfrac{7}{10} =$

20) $\dfrac{3}{9} \times \dfrac{1}{3} =$

21) $\dfrac{1}{11} \times \dfrac{10}{12} =$

22) $\dfrac{1}{2} \times \dfrac{8}{12} =$

23) $\dfrac{3}{4} \times \dfrac{1}{2} =$

24) $\dfrac{5}{6} \times \dfrac{3}{9} =$

25) $\dfrac{1}{12} \times \dfrac{4}{6} =$

26) $\dfrac{10}{11} \times \dfrac{3}{4} =$

27) $\dfrac{5}{10} \times \dfrac{3}{6} =$

28) $\dfrac{1}{4} \times \dfrac{5}{6} =$

29) $\dfrac{4}{11} \times \dfrac{2}{3} =$

30) $\dfrac{4}{5} \times \dfrac{3}{6} =$

1) $\dfrac{1}{7} \times \dfrac{1}{8} =$

2) $\dfrac{1}{2} \times \dfrac{1}{7} =$

3) $\dfrac{2}{8} \times \dfrac{10}{11} =$

4) $\dfrac{2}{7} \times \dfrac{3}{12} =$

5) $\dfrac{2}{6} \times \dfrac{5}{10} =$

6) $\dfrac{4}{11} \times \dfrac{7}{9} =$

7) $\dfrac{3}{4} \times \dfrac{2}{6} =$

8) $\dfrac{3}{4} \times \dfrac{1}{2} =$

9) $\dfrac{2}{9} \times \dfrac{1}{2} =$

10) $\dfrac{2}{9} \times \dfrac{3}{4} =$

11) $\dfrac{1}{12} \times \dfrac{4}{5} =$

12) $\dfrac{5}{9} \times \dfrac{3}{10} =$

13) $\dfrac{4}{10} \times \dfrac{1}{2} =$

14) $\dfrac{4}{5} \times \dfrac{7}{9} =$

15) $\dfrac{10}{11} \times \dfrac{1}{8} =$

16) $\dfrac{3}{7} \times \dfrac{3}{12} =$

17) $\dfrac{4}{11} \times \dfrac{8}{9} =$

18) $\dfrac{3}{4} \times \dfrac{1}{6} =$

19) $\dfrac{4}{5} \times \dfrac{1}{3} =$

20) $\dfrac{2}{7} \times \dfrac{6}{11} =$

21) $\dfrac{1}{2} \times \dfrac{2}{8} =$

22) $\dfrac{2}{12} \times \dfrac{3}{4} =$

23) $\dfrac{5}{12} \times \dfrac{6}{9} =$

24) $\dfrac{1}{10} \times \dfrac{1}{2} =$

25) $\dfrac{1}{5} \times \dfrac{2}{11} =$

26) $\dfrac{6}{7} \times \dfrac{5}{12} =$

27) $\dfrac{1}{8} \times \dfrac{1}{11} =$

28) $\dfrac{1}{3} \times \dfrac{1}{11} =$

29) $\dfrac{3}{8} \times \dfrac{5}{10} =$

30) $\dfrac{2}{4} \times \dfrac{3}{11} =$

Level 8

Fractions

Dividing fractions
(denominators 2-10)

1) $\dfrac{4}{5} \div \dfrac{4}{6} =$

2) $\dfrac{7}{9} \div \dfrac{1}{2} =$

3) $\dfrac{5}{9} \div \dfrac{4}{6} =$

4) $\dfrac{1}{2} \div \dfrac{1}{7} =$

5) $\dfrac{8}{10} \div \dfrac{1}{9} =$

6) $\dfrac{2}{5} \div \dfrac{1}{3} =$

7) $\dfrac{3}{7} \div \dfrac{3}{8} =$

8) $\dfrac{2}{3} \div \dfrac{5}{7} =$

9) $\dfrac{2}{4} \div \dfrac{2}{5} =$

10) $\dfrac{1}{2} \div \dfrac{2}{3} =$

11) $\dfrac{2}{6} \div \dfrac{3}{7} =$

12) $\dfrac{7}{9} \div \dfrac{5}{8} =$

13) $\dfrac{3}{8} \div \dfrac{1}{9} =$

14) $\dfrac{5}{8} \div \dfrac{5}{6} =$

15) $\dfrac{1}{2} \div \dfrac{1}{7} =$

16) $\dfrac{2}{3} \div \dfrac{4}{5} =$

17) $\dfrac{2}{5} \div \dfrac{1}{2} =$

18) $\dfrac{4}{6} \div \dfrac{1}{5} =$

19) $\dfrac{7}{8} \div \dfrac{2}{5} =$

20) $\dfrac{3}{5} \div \dfrac{1}{2} =$

21) $\dfrac{3}{6} \div \dfrac{6}{9} =$

22) $\dfrac{6}{8} \div \dfrac{2}{5} =$

23) $\dfrac{1}{3} \div \dfrac{3}{8} =$

24) $\dfrac{6}{10} \div \dfrac{5}{6} =$

25) $\dfrac{1}{8} \div \dfrac{2}{5} =$

26) $\dfrac{1}{5} \div \dfrac{1}{3} =$

27) $\dfrac{2}{4} \div \dfrac{2}{6} =$

28) $\dfrac{4}{9} \div \dfrac{9}{10} =$

29) $\dfrac{5}{6} \div \dfrac{1}{9} =$

30) $\dfrac{2}{3} \div \dfrac{1}{4} =$

1) $\dfrac{1}{2} \div \dfrac{1}{3} =$

2) $\dfrac{3}{5} \div \dfrac{1}{2} =$

3) $\dfrac{1}{7} \div \dfrac{5}{10} =$

4) $\dfrac{5}{9} \div \dfrac{1}{4} =$

5) $\dfrac{5}{9} \div \dfrac{1}{2} =$

6) $\dfrac{3}{4} \div \dfrac{5}{8} =$

7) $\dfrac{7}{9} \div \dfrac{1}{2} =$

8) $\dfrac{5}{8} \div \dfrac{1}{2} =$

9) $\dfrac{4}{7} \div \dfrac{5}{9} =$

10) $\dfrac{1}{3} \div \dfrac{5}{6} =$

11) $\dfrac{9}{10} \div \dfrac{3}{6} =$

12) $\dfrac{2}{3} \div \dfrac{1}{5} =$

13) $\dfrac{1}{4} \div \dfrac{2}{9} =$

14) $\dfrac{3}{10} \div \dfrac{1}{6} =$

15) $\dfrac{1}{2} \div \dfrac{7}{9} =$

16) $\dfrac{6}{8} \div \dfrac{5}{6} =$

17) $\dfrac{1}{2} \div \dfrac{2}{3} =$

18) $\dfrac{1}{6} \div \dfrac{1}{2} =$

19) $\dfrac{3}{5} \div \dfrac{1}{2} =$

20) $\dfrac{3}{6} \div \dfrac{9}{10} =$

21) $\dfrac{1}{2} \div \dfrac{8}{9} =$

22) $\dfrac{4}{6} \div \dfrac{1}{5} =$

23) $\dfrac{5}{6} \div \dfrac{4}{5} =$

24) $\dfrac{3}{4} \div \dfrac{4}{8} =$

25) $\dfrac{7}{8} \div \dfrac{1}{2} =$

26) $\dfrac{1}{6} \div \dfrac{1}{5} =$

27) $\dfrac{3}{10} \div \dfrac{1}{2} =$

28) $\dfrac{5}{7} \div \dfrac{1}{5} =$

29) $\dfrac{7}{9} \div \dfrac{7}{8} =$

30) $\dfrac{5}{10} \div \dfrac{2}{7} =$

1) $\dfrac{6}{7} \div \dfrac{4}{6} =$

2) $\dfrac{7}{10} \div \dfrac{3}{6} =$

3) $\dfrac{1}{2} \div \dfrac{7}{8} =$

4) $\dfrac{1}{2} \div \dfrac{2}{9} =$

5) $\dfrac{2}{4} \div \dfrac{2}{5} =$

6) $\dfrac{5}{8} \div \dfrac{7}{9} =$

7) $\dfrac{5}{8} \div \dfrac{1}{5} =$

8) $\dfrac{2}{4} \div \dfrac{1}{5} =$

9) $\dfrac{2}{3} \div \dfrac{4}{10} =$

10) $\dfrac{2}{8} \div \dfrac{7}{9} =$

11) $\dfrac{5}{7} \div \dfrac{7}{9} =$

12) $\dfrac{5}{7} \div \dfrac{1}{2} =$

13) $\dfrac{1}{4} \div \dfrac{3}{10} =$

14) $\dfrac{4}{10} \div \dfrac{6}{7} =$

15) $\dfrac{3}{4} \div \dfrac{7}{8} =$

16) $\dfrac{2}{7} \div \dfrac{4}{5} =$

17) $\dfrac{1}{2} \div \dfrac{3}{5} =$

18) $\dfrac{4}{7} \div \dfrac{2}{3} =$

19) $\dfrac{7}{8} \div \dfrac{6}{10} =$

20) $\dfrac{1}{9} \div \dfrac{3}{8} =$

21) $\dfrac{4}{5} \div \dfrac{3}{10} =$

22) $\dfrac{1}{6} \div \dfrac{2}{7} =$

23) $\dfrac{3}{8} \div \dfrac{4}{5} =$

24) $\dfrac{1}{2} \div \dfrac{6}{10} =$

25) $\dfrac{1}{2} \div \dfrac{5}{6} =$

26) $\dfrac{5}{8} \div \dfrac{5}{7} =$

27) $\dfrac{3}{7} \div \dfrac{7}{10} =$

28) $\dfrac{4}{5} \div \dfrac{3}{4} =$

29) $\dfrac{4}{5} \div \dfrac{9}{10} =$

30) $\dfrac{7}{9} \div \dfrac{2}{3} =$

1) $\frac{3}{4} \div \frac{4}{7} =$

2) $\frac{1}{10} \div \frac{1}{2} =$

3) $\frac{5}{7} \div \frac{8}{10} =$

4) $\frac{2}{7} \div \frac{8}{10} =$

5) $\frac{1}{8} \div \frac{3}{9} =$

6) $\frac{6}{9} \div \frac{4}{10} =$

7) $\frac{3}{10} \div \frac{5}{8} =$

8) $\frac{5}{7} \div \frac{7}{9} =$

9) $\frac{2}{9} \div \frac{1}{5} =$

10) $\frac{8}{9} \div \frac{1}{5} =$

11) $\frac{2}{6} \div \frac{2}{3} =$

12) $\frac{1}{5} \div \frac{1}{6} =$

13) $\frac{6}{10} \div \frac{3}{4} =$

14) $\frac{1}{8} \div \frac{1}{2} =$

15) $\frac{6}{9} \div \frac{5}{6} =$

16) $\frac{4}{10} \div \frac{1}{3} =$

17) $\frac{5}{10} \div \frac{4}{9} =$

18) $\frac{2}{8} \div \frac{4}{5} =$

19) $\frac{2}{4} \div \frac{2}{6} =$

20) $\frac{1}{3} \div \frac{6}{9} =$

21) $\frac{5}{8} \div \frac{1}{5} =$

22) $\frac{2}{3} \div \frac{2}{5} =$

23) $\frac{1}{3} \div \frac{2}{8} =$

24) $\frac{2}{3} \div \frac{3}{4} =$

25) $\frac{5}{6} \div \frac{1}{2} =$

26) $\frac{5}{9} \div \frac{1}{2} =$

27) $\frac{1}{4} \div \frac{1}{6} =$

28) $\frac{2}{8} \div \frac{1}{7} =$

29) $\frac{2}{5} \div \frac{1}{6} =$

30) $\frac{5}{7} \div \frac{5}{8} =$

1) $\dfrac{1}{2} \div \dfrac{1}{5} =$

2) $\dfrac{1}{3} \div \dfrac{2}{7} =$

3) $\dfrac{1}{3} \div \dfrac{1}{5} =$

4) $\dfrac{1}{2} \div \dfrac{1}{9} =$

5) $\dfrac{1}{3} \div \dfrac{2}{5} =$

6) $\dfrac{1}{3} \div \dfrac{3}{10} =$

7) $\dfrac{6}{9} \div \dfrac{1}{10} =$

8) $\dfrac{1}{3} \div \dfrac{4}{8} =$

9) $\dfrac{1}{4} \div \dfrac{3}{5} =$

10) $\dfrac{2}{7} \div \dfrac{5}{8} =$

11) $\dfrac{2}{3} \div \dfrac{6}{10} =$

12) $\dfrac{2}{10} \div \dfrac{7}{8} =$

13) $\dfrac{1}{3} \div \dfrac{4}{7} =$

14) $\dfrac{1}{3} \div \dfrac{5}{9} =$

15) $\dfrac{1}{8} \div \dfrac{6}{10} =$

16) $\dfrac{4}{8} \div \dfrac{1}{5} =$

17) $\dfrac{4}{6} \div \dfrac{1}{2} =$

18) $\dfrac{3}{10} \div \dfrac{3}{6} =$

19) $\dfrac{1}{4} \div \dfrac{4}{6} =$

20) $\dfrac{3}{8} \div \dfrac{3}{6} =$

21) $\dfrac{8}{9} \div \dfrac{2}{4} =$

22) $\dfrac{1}{4} \div \dfrac{1}{2} =$

23) $\dfrac{1}{3} \div \dfrac{4}{10} =$

24) $\dfrac{1}{4} \div \dfrac{3}{5} =$

25) $\dfrac{1}{2} \div \dfrac{1}{7} =$

26) $\dfrac{1}{2} \div \dfrac{2}{6} =$

27) $\dfrac{1}{2} \div \dfrac{3}{8} =$

28) $\dfrac{4}{5} \div \dfrac{9}{10} =$

29) $\dfrac{1}{2} \div \dfrac{7}{9} =$

30) $\dfrac{5}{8} \div \dfrac{1}{2} =$

1) $\dfrac{1}{4} \div \dfrac{4}{6} =$

2) $\dfrac{1}{2} \div \dfrac{6}{10} =$

3) $\dfrac{2}{4} \div \dfrac{4}{10} =$

4) $\dfrac{2}{6} \div \dfrac{1}{5} =$

5) $\dfrac{4}{10} \div \dfrac{1}{3} =$

6) $\dfrac{1}{2} \div \dfrac{3}{9} =$

7) $\dfrac{5}{7} \div \dfrac{5}{10} =$

8) $\dfrac{3}{10} \div \dfrac{4}{8} =$

9) $\dfrac{1}{3} \div \dfrac{1}{8} =$

10) $\dfrac{3}{5} \div \dfrac{7}{10} =$

11) $\dfrac{3}{6} \div \dfrac{4}{9} =$

12) $\dfrac{1}{5} \div \dfrac{5}{9} =$

13) $\dfrac{4}{9} \div \dfrac{2}{4} =$

14) $\dfrac{1}{6} \div \dfrac{1}{3} =$

15) $\dfrac{3}{7} \div \dfrac{5}{10} =$

16) $\dfrac{1}{9} \div \dfrac{6}{8} =$

17) $\dfrac{3}{5} \div \dfrac{1}{3} =$

18) $\dfrac{4}{8} \div \dfrac{8}{10} =$

19) $\dfrac{2}{4} \div \dfrac{4}{7} =$

20) $\dfrac{3}{10} \div \dfrac{3}{4} =$

21) $\dfrac{3}{8} \div \dfrac{2}{5} =$

22) $\dfrac{2}{10} \div \dfrac{2}{4} =$

23) $\dfrac{5}{10} \div \dfrac{1}{3} =$

24) $\dfrac{1}{5} \div \dfrac{1}{2} =$

25) $\dfrac{4}{5} \div \dfrac{1}{2} =$

26) $\dfrac{7}{8} \div \dfrac{2}{7} =$

27) $\dfrac{6}{9} \div \dfrac{5}{7} =$

28) $\dfrac{2}{3} \div \dfrac{1}{4} =$

29) $\dfrac{1}{2} \div \dfrac{2}{7} =$

30) $\dfrac{3}{6} \div \dfrac{2}{3} =$

Level 9

Decimals

Adding 3-digit decimals
(missing addends)

1)
```
      ____
  +  3.476
  ───────
     5.802
```

2)
```
      ____
  +  2.211
  ───────
     6.174
```

3)
```
      ____
  +  3.612
  ───────
     6.172
```

4)
```
      ____
  +  1.331
  ───────
     4.683
```

5)
```
      ____
  +  3.625
  ───────
     4.734
```

6)
```
      ____
  +  0.284
  ───────
     1.140
```

7)
```
      ____
  +  1.816
  ───────
     4.404
```

8)
```
      ____
  +  3.657
  ───────
     4.689
```

9)
```
      ____
  +  1.396
  ───────
     6.380
```

10)
```
      ____
  +  3.742
  ───────
     4.402
```

11)
```
      ____
  +  2.609
  ───────
     2.932
```

12)
```
      ____
  +  1.730
  ───────
     2.199
```

13)
```
      ____
  +  0.741
  ───────
     1.686
```

14)
```
      ____
  +  0.923
  ───────
     5.446
```

15)
```
      ____
  +  1.906
  ───────
     4.937
```

16)
```
      ____
  +  3.104
  ───────
     5.044
```

17)
```
      ____
  +  1.397
  ───────
     5.056
```

18)
```
      ____
  +  0.294
  ───────
     0.852
```

19)
```
      ____
  +  2.886
  ───────
     6.074
```

20)
```
      ____
  +  0.813
  ───────
     2.840
```

21)
```
      ____
  +  3.492
  ───────
     5.476
```

22)
```
      ____
  +  1.568
  ───────
     4.714
```

23)
```
      ____
  +  0.519
  ───────
     4.067
```

24)
```
      ____
  +  1.810
  ───────
     3.149
```

25)
```
      ____
  +  2.278
  ───────
     3.339
```

26)
```
      ____
  +  1.597
  ───────
     2.154
```

27)
```
      ____
  +  0.167
  ───────
     4.881
```

28)
```
      ____
  +  2.223
  ───────
     6.315
```

29)
```
      ____
  +  2.853
  ───────
     4.560
```

30)
```
      ____
  +  3.192
  ───────
     6.915
```

31)
```
      ____
  +  1.788
  ───────
     2.153
```

32)
```
      ____
  +  0.855
  ───────
     0.989
```

1)
```
      [    ]
  +  0.955
  ─────────
     1.979
```

2)
```
      [    ]
  +  2.307
  ─────────
     5.778
```

3)
```
      [    ]
  +  3.550
  ─────────
     4.941
```

4)
```
      [    ]
  +  1.580
  ─────────
     5.589
```

5)
```
      [    ]
  +  0.984
  ─────────
     3.674
```

6)
```
      [    ]
  +  2.258
  ─────────
     6.965
```

7)
```
      [    ]
  +  3.531
  ─────────
     8.394
```

8)
```
      [    ]
  +  2.588
  ─────────
     7.188
```

9)
```
      [    ]
  +  1.916
  ─────────
     6.242
```

10)
```
      [    ]
  +  1.759
  ─────────
     4.561
```

11)
```
      [    ]
  +  0.982
  ─────────
     3.081
```

12)
```
      [    ]
  +  0.381
  ─────────
     2.666
```

13)
```
      [    ]
  +  3.908
  ─────────
     5.176
```

14)
```
      [    ]
  +  2.657
  ─────────
     6.967
```

15)
```
      [    ]
  +  0.853
  ─────────
     1.387
```

16)
```
      [    ]
  +  1.048
  ─────────
     3.112
```

17)
```
      [    ]
  +  0.379
  ─────────
     2.539
```

18)
```
      [    ]
  +  0.987
  ─────────
     3.185
```

19)
```
      [    ]
  +  3.446
  ─────────
     8.264
```

20)
```
      [    ]
  +  2.179
  ─────────
     4.439
```

21)
```
      [    ]
  +  0.223
  ─────────
     5.201
```

22)
```
      [    ]
  +  3.285
  ─────────
     6.310
```

23)
```
      [    ]
  +  3.713
  ─────────
     8.708
```

24)
```
      [    ]
  +  0.185
  ─────────
     1.190
```

25)
```
      [    ]
  +  1.507
  ─────────
     1.577
```

26)
```
      [    ]
  +  1.506
  ─────────
     4.387
```

27)
```
      [    ]
  +  0.375
  ─────────
     2.211
```

28)
```
      [    ]
  +  2.163
  ─────────
     4.650
```

29)
```
      [    ]
  +  3.010
  ─────────
     6.317
```

30)
```
      [    ]
  +  1.322
  ─────────
     2.391
```

31)
```
      [    ]
  +  1.989
  ─────────
     3.870
```

32)
```
      [    ]
  +  1.661
  ─────────
     5.543
```

1)
```
      ____
   +  2.316
   ───────
      4.903
```

2)
```
      ____
   +  0.538
   ───────
      4.600
```

3)
```
      ____
   +  2.063
   ───────
      3.698
```

4)
```
      ____
   +  3.440
   ───────
      7.651
```

5)
```
      ____
   +  2.797
   ───────
      3.371
```

6)
```
      ____
   +  1.961
   ───────
      6.743
```

7)
```
      ____
   +  1.088
   ───────
      3.866
```

8)
```
      ____
   +  0.429
   ───────
      1.572
```

9)
```
      ____
   +  2.762
   ───────
      4.332
```

10)
```
      ____
   +  1.490
   ───────
      6.127
```

11)
```
      ____
   +  2.850
   ───────
      6.726
```

12)
```
      ____
   +  3.165
   ───────
      8.142
```

13)
```
      ____
   +  3.761
   ───────
      7.529
```

14)
```
      ____
   +  3.291
   ───────
      3.932
```

15)
```
      ____
   +  2.069
   ───────
      6.580
```

16)
```
      ____
   +  2.748
   ───────
      5.282
```

17)
```
      ____
   +  1.903
   ───────
      4.223
```

18)
```
      ____
   +  1.932
   ───────
      3.722
```

19)
```
      ____
   +  3.493
   ───────
      4.881
```

20)
```
      ____
   +  0.419
   ───────
      0.823
```

21)
```
      ____
   +  1.445
   ───────
      2.251
```

22)
```
      ____
   +  2.141
   ───────
      5.083
```

23)
```
      ____
   +  0.919
   ───────
      4.106
```

24)
```
      ____
   +  3.987
   ───────
      6.081
```

25)
```
      ____
   +  1.768
   ───────
      1.853
```

26)
```
      ____
   +  3.272
   ───────
      5.876
```

27)
```
      ____
   +  2.390
   ───────
      4.995
```

28)
```
      ____
   +  0.236
   ───────
      2.548
```

29)
```
      ____
   +  0.142
   ───────
      2.244
```

30)
```
      ____
   +  0.847
   ───────
      4.973
```

31)
```
      ____
   +  2.854
   ───────
      5.663
```

32)
```
      ____
   +  2.637
   ───────
      7.526
```

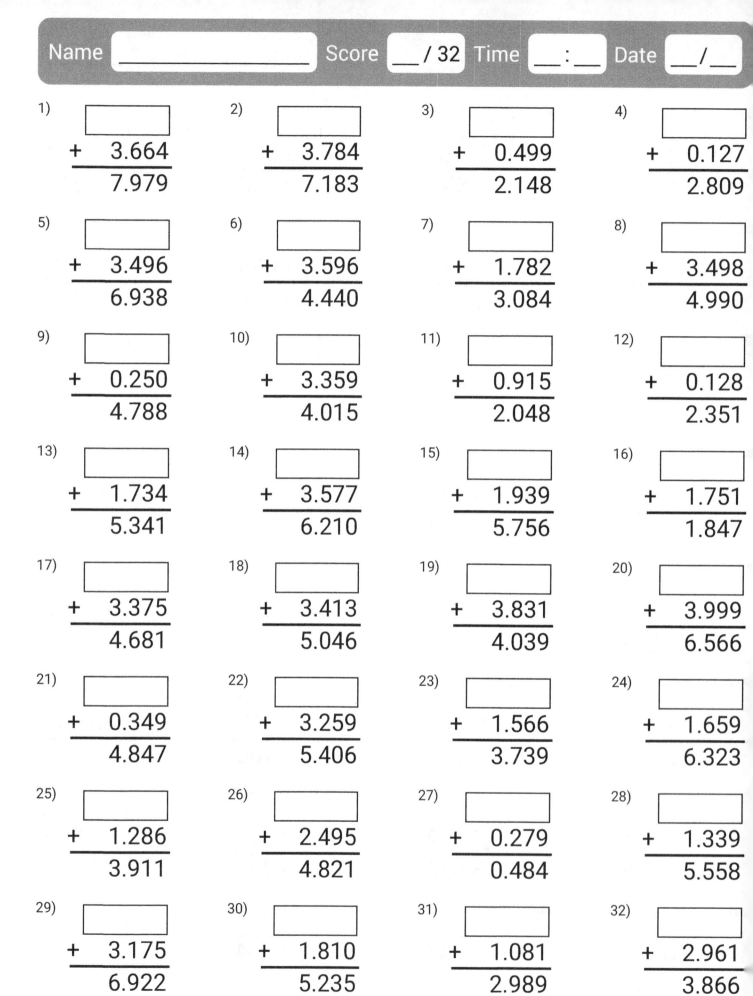

1)
```
      ____
  +  3.664
  ─────────
     7.979
```

2)
```
      ____
  +  3.784
  ─────────
     7.183
```

3)
```
      ____
  +  0.499
  ─────────
     2.148
```

4)
```
      ____
  +  0.127
  ─────────
     2.809
```

5)
```
      ____
  +  3.496
  ─────────
     6.938
```

6)
```
      ____
  +  3.596
  ─────────
     4.440
```

7)
```
      ____
  +  1.782
  ─────────
     3.084
```

8)
```
      ____
  +  3.498
  ─────────
     4.990
```

9)
```
      ____
  +  0.250
  ─────────
     4.788
```

10)
```
      ____
  +  3.359
  ─────────
     4.015
```

11)
```
      ____
  +  0.915
  ─────────
     2.048
```

12)
```
      ____
  +  0.128
  ─────────
     2.351
```

13)
```
      ____
  +  1.734
  ─────────
     5.341
```

14)
```
      ____
  +  3.577
  ─────────
     6.210
```

15)
```
      ____
  +  1.939
  ─────────
     5.756
```

16)
```
      ____
  +  1.751
  ─────────
     1.847
```

17)
```
      ____
  +  3.375
  ─────────
     4.681
```

18)
```
      ____
  +  3.413
  ─────────
     5.046
```

19)
```
      ____
  +  3.831
  ─────────
     4.039
```

20)
```
      ____
  +  3.999
  ─────────
     6.566
```

21)
```
      ____
  +  0.349
  ─────────
     4.847
```

22)
```
      ____
  +  3.259
  ─────────
     5.406
```

23)
```
      ____
  +  1.566
  ─────────
     3.739
```

24)
```
      ____
  +  1.659
  ─────────
     6.323
```

25)
```
      ____
  +  1.286
  ─────────
     3.911
```

26)
```
      ____
  +  2.495
  ─────────
     4.821
```

27)
```
      ____
  +  0.279
  ─────────
     0.484
```

28)
```
      ____
  +  1.339
  ─────────
     5.558
```

29)
```
      ____
  +  3.175
  ─────────
     6.922
```

30)
```
      ____
  +  1.810
  ─────────
     5.235
```

31)
```
      ____
  +  1.081
  ─────────
     2.989
```

32)
```
      ____
  +  2.961
  ─────────
     3.866
```

1)
```
      _____
  +    0.878
  ----------
       3.425
```

2)
```
      _____
  +    3.582
  ----------
       4.022
```

3)
```
      _____
  +    2.149
  ----------
       3.691
```

4)
```
      _____
  +    3.328
  ----------
       5.650
```

5)
```
      _____
  +    2.593
  ----------
       2.991
```

6)
```
      _____
  +    1.756
  ----------
       5.844
```

7)
```
      _____
  +    0.823
  ----------
       1.624
```

8)
```
      _____
  +    3.345
  ----------
       3.982
```

9)
```
      _____
  +    3.884
  ----------
       6.283
```

10)
```
      _____
  +    1.231
  ----------
       4.135
```

11)
```
      _____
  +    2.328
  ----------
       6.153
```

12)
```
      _____
  +    2.739
  ----------
       4.361
```

13)
```
      _____
  +    3.057
  ----------
       4.828
```

14)
```
      _____
  +    3.573
  ----------
       4.236
```

15)
```
      _____
  +    1.400
  ----------
       4.630
```

16)
```
      _____
  +    3.885
  ----------
       5.311
```

17)
```
      _____
  +    3.598
  ----------
       7.916
```

18)
```
      _____
  +    0.597
  ----------
       3.116
```

19)
```
      _____
  +    3.152
  ----------
       6.556
```

20)
```
      _____
  +    1.550
  ----------
       1.689
```

21)
```
      _____
  +    2.218
  ----------
       6.284
```

22)
```
      _____
  +    2.850
  ----------
       6.199
```

23)
```
      _____
  +    0.196
  ----------
       1.384
```

24)
```
      _____
  +    1.023
  ----------
       5.470
```

25)
```
      _____
  +    2.773
  ----------
       7.256
```

26)
```
      _____
  +    2.925
  ----------
       7.100
```

27)
```
      _____
  +    3.739
  ----------
       6.645
```

28)
```
      _____
  +    0.252
  ----------
       0.332
```

29)
```
      _____
  +    0.108
  ----------
       4.447
```

30)
```
      _____
  +    2.373
  ----------
       6.646
```

31)
```
      _____
  +    2.042
  ----------
       6.175
```

32)
```
      _____
  +    1.508
  ----------
       4.419
```

1)
```
        [    ]
   +   1.877
   ─────────
       3.165
```

2)
```
        [    ]
   +   0.700
   ─────────
       5.262
```

3)
```
        [    ]
   +   0.670
   ─────────
       1.261
```

4)
```
        [    ]
   +   2.700
   ─────────
       3.060
```

5)
```
        [    ]
   +   3.618
   ─────────
       5.696
```

6)
```
        [    ]
   +   3.047
   ─────────
       4.457
```

7)
```
        [    ]
   +   0.203
   ─────────
       3.930
```

8)
```
        [    ]
   +   1.337
   ─────────
       4.660
```

9)
```
        [    ]
   +   3.667
   ─────────
       8.438
```

10)
```
        [    ]
   +   3.936
   ─────────
       4.258
```

11)
```
        [    ]
   +   2.478
   ─────────
       7.424
```

12)
```
        [    ]
   +   0.736
   ─────────
       2.338
```

13)
```
        [    ]
   +   1.429
   ─────────
       6.169
```

14)
```
        [    ]
   +   1.249
   ─────────
       2.950
```

15)
```
        [    ]
   +   0.630
   ─────────
       2.933
```

16)
```
        [    ]
   +   3.279
   ─────────
       3.902
```

17)
```
        [    ]
   +   3.686
   ─────────
       5.288
```

18)
```
        [    ]
   +   1.386
   ─────────
       2.358
```

19)
```
        [    ]
   +   1.238
   ─────────
       2.864
```

20)
```
        [    ]
   +   2.724
   ─────────
       6.796
```

21)
```
        [    ]
   +   2.030
   ─────────
       7.010
```

22)
```
        [    ]
   +   0.709
   ─────────
       3.143
```

23)
```
        [    ]
   +   1.819
   ─────────
       2.702
```

24)
```
        [    ]
   +   1.527
   ─────────
       2.990
```

25)
```
        [    ]
   +   2.811
   ─────────
       5.032
```

26)
```
        [    ]
   +   2.053
   ─────────
       2.991
```

27)
```
        [    ]
   +   1.339
   ─────────
       5.458
```

28)
```
        [    ]
   +   0.991
   ─────────
       1.599
```

29)
```
        [    ]
   +   0.673
   ─────────
       2.406
```

30)
```
        [    ]
   +   3.642
   ─────────
       5.618
```

31)
```
        [    ]
   +   0.804
   ─────────
       2.546
```

32)
```
        [    ]
   +   0.883
   ─────────
       2.047
```

Level 10

Decimals

Subtracting 3-digit decimals
(missing subtrahends)

1) 4.089
− [ ]
3.408

2) 3.239
− [ ]
0.006

3) 0.818
− [ ]
0.150

4) 3.895
− [ ]
0.021

5) 3.958
− [ ]
3.375

6) 1.846
− [ ]
1.489

7) 4.063
− [ ]
0.867

8) 4.941
− [ ]
2.822

9) 1.569
− [ ]
1.381

10) 3.730
− [ ]
0.604

11) 2.368
− [ ]
0.507

12) 0.878
− [ ]
0.279

13) 3.673
− [ ]
0.457

14) 3.832
− [ ]
0.779

15) 2.852
− [ ]
0.347

16) 2.483
− [ ]
1.134

17) 3.574
− [ ]
1.478

18) 4.121
− [ ]
2.673

19) 3.792
− [ ]
0.887

20) 3.356
− [ ]
0.498

21) 3.501
− [ ]
1.235

22) 4.669
− [ ]
3.734

23) 4.259
− [ ]
3.624

24) 1.729
− [ ]
0.356

25) 2.624
− [ ]
0.018

26) 3.944
− [ ]
2.721

27) 2.395
− [ ]
0.251

28) 2.900
− [ ]
0.531

29) 4.372
− [ ]
2.925

30) 4.945
− [ ]
3.363

31) 4.199
− [ ]
1.596

32) 1.940
− [ ]
0.352

1) 2.720
  − [ ]
  ___
  1.223

2) 1.187
  − [ ]
  ___
  0.834

3) 4.045
  − [ ]
  ___
  0.681

4) 4.103
  − [ ]
  ___
  1.697

5) 1.845
  − [ ]
  ___
  0.903

6) 3.262
  − [ ]
  ___
  2.581

7) 2.018
  − [ ]
  ___
  0.331

8) 2.614
  − [ ]
  ___
  0.661

9) 3.610
  − [ ]
  ___
  2.890

10) 1.448
  − [ ]
  ___
  0.973

11) 2.890
  − [ ]
  ___
  1.192

12) 2.228
  − [ ]
  ___
  1.329

13) 1.367
  − [ ]
  ___
  0.396

14) 4.550
  − [ ]
  ___
  3.178

15) 2.201
  − [ ]
  ___
  1.617

16) 4.796
  − [ ]
  ___
  3.446

17) 1.638
  − [ ]
  ___
  0.678

18) 3.999
  − [ ]
  ___
  1.775

19) 4.351
  − [ ]
  ___
  1.425

20) 2.430
  − [ ]
  ___
  1.648

21) 3.634
  − [ ]
  ___
  2.555

22) 4.264
  − [ ]
  ___
  2.698

23) 4.649
  − [ ]
  ___
  3.769

24) 4.986
  − [ ]
  ___
  2.867

25) 3.371
  − [ ]
  ___
  3.202

26) 1.715
  − [ ]
  ___
  0.701

27) 2.309
  − [ ]
  ___
  1.505

28) 4.624
  − [ ]
  ___
  4.341

29) 3.736
  − [ ]
  ___
  0.355

30) 1.865
  − [ ]
  ___
  1.279

31) 2.517
  − [ ]
  ___
  1.789

32) 0.342
  − [ ]
  ___
  0.106

1)   3.773
   − [ ]
   ────────
     0.985

2)   1.164
   − [ ]
   ────────
     0.319

3)   3.659
   − [ ]
   ────────
     3.487

4)   4.874
   − [ ]
   ────────
     1.783

5)   4.479
   − [ ]
   ────────
     1.710

6)   2.196
   − [ ]
   ────────
     1.852

7)   2.085
   − [ ]
   ────────
     1.135

8)   2.965
   − [ ]
   ────────
     2.914

9)   2.950
   − [ ]
   ────────
     0.700

10) 4.874
   − [ ]
   ────────
     2.933

11) 1.618
   − [ ]
   ────────
     0.524

12) 3.407
   − [ ]
   ────────
     3.207

13) 3.696
   − [ ]
   ────────
     1.304

14) 4.953
   − [ ]
   ────────
     3.867

15) 4.778
   − [ ]
   ────────
     4.718

16) 2.911
   − [ ]
   ────────
     1.043

17) 3.746
   − [ ]
   ────────
     0.301

18) 4.657
   − [ ]
   ────────
     2.346

19) 3.740
   − [ ]
   ────────
     3.422

20) 3.105
   − [ ]
   ────────
     2.398

21) 4.993
   − [ ]
   ────────
     3.482

22) 3.217
   − [ ]
   ────────
     0.573

23) 1.226
   − [ ]
   ────────
     1.026

24) 1.539
   − [ ]
   ────────
     0.126

25) 4.380
   − [ ]
   ────────
     4.070

26) 4.505
   − [ ]
   ────────
     2.096

27) 3.919
   − [ ]
   ────────
     3.195

28) 3.908
   − [ ]
   ────────
     1.698

29) 1.412
   − [ ]
   ────────
     0.528

30) 3.273
   − [ ]
   ────────
     2.035

31) 4.916
   − [ ]
   ────────
     3.393

32) 1.130
   − [ ]
   ────────
     0.033

1)
3.341
− [ ]
1.962

2)
4.544
− [ ]
0.835

3)
2.995
− [ ]
1.110

4)
3.470
− [ ]
2.894

5)
2.396
− [ ]
0.546

6)
4.687
− [ ]
2.566

7)
3.618
− [ ]
1.260

8)
3.316
− [ ]
0.989

9)
0.567
− [ ]
0.135

10)
2.695
− [ ]
1.091

11)
3.983
− [ ]
3.200

12)
3.575
− [ ]
1.093

13)
4.805
− [ ]
2.009

14)
4.404
− [ ]
0.644

15)
4.054
− [ ]
1.500

16)
3.565
− [ ]
3.512

17)
4.320
− [ ]
1.076

18)
3.628
− [ ]
0.072

19)
3.750
− [ ]
1.673

20)
3.358
− [ ]
0.479

21)
1.742
− [ ]
1.527

22)
2.729
− [ ]
2.231

23)
4.362
− [ ]
3.477

24)
0.930
− [ ]
0.798

25)
3.869
− [ ]
2.594

26)
2.419
− [ ]
1.196

27)
3.726
− [ ]
3.627

28)
3.802
− [ ]
1.069

29)
4.665
− [ ]
3.370

30)
2.842
− [ ]
1.502

31)
3.033
− [ ]
1.246

32)
1.614
− [ ]
0.673

1) 0.975
   − [＿＿]
   ‾‾‾‾‾‾
    0.722

2) 4.892
   − [＿＿]
   ‾‾‾‾‾‾
    2.872

3) 4.681
   − [＿＿]
   ‾‾‾‾‾‾
    2.116

4) 4.686
   − [＿＿]
   ‾‾‾‾‾‾
    0.992

5) 4.400
   − [＿＿]
   ‾‾‾‾‾‾
    4.224

6) 4.623
   − [＿＿]
   ‾‾‾‾‾‾
    1.492

7) 3.039
   − [＿＿]
   ‾‾‾‾‾‾
    0.595

8) 0.693
   − [＿＿]
   ‾‾‾‾‾‾
    0.614

9) 2.574
   − [＿＿]
   ‾‾‾‾‾‾
    0.841

10) 1.350
   − [＿＿]
   ‾‾‾‾‾‾
    1.212

11) 2.901
   − [＿＿]
   ‾‾‾‾‾‾
    1.483

12) 2.722
   − [＿＿]
   ‾‾‾‾‾‾
    2.383

13) 4.614
   − [＿＿]
   ‾‾‾‾‾‾
    4.305

14) 3.536
   − [＿＿]
   ‾‾‾‾‾‾
    1.236

15) 3.222
   − [＿＿]
   ‾‾‾‾‾‾
    1.487

16) 4.201
   − [＿＿]
   ‾‾‾‾‾‾
    3.667

17) 3.744
   − [＿＿]
   ‾‾‾‾‾‾
    0.445

18) 2.544
   − [＿＿]
   ‾‾‾‾‾‾
    2.281

19) 3.915
   − [＿＿]
   ‾‾‾‾‾‾
    0.221

20) 4.512
   − [＿＿]
   ‾‾‾‾‾‾
    2.956

21) 3.724
   − [＿＿]
   ‾‾‾‾‾‾
    1.358

22) 3.319
   − [＿＿]
   ‾‾‾‾‾‾
    0.789

23) 3.669
   − [＿＿]
   ‾‾‾‾‾‾
    0.488

24) 4.561
   − [＿＿]
   ‾‾‾‾‾‾
    3.064

25) 3.006
   − [＿＿]
   ‾‾‾‾‾‾
    0.054

26) 3.331
   − [＿＿]
   ‾‾‾‾‾‾
    2.133

27) 3.637
   − [＿＿]
   ‾‾‾‾‾‾
    2.240

28) 4.303
   − [＿＿]
   ‾‾‾‾‾‾
    2.826

29) 2.654
   − [＿＿]
   ‾‾‾‾‾‾
    0.221

30) 1.315
   − [＿＿]
   ‾‾‾‾‾‾
    0.455

31) 2.835
   − [＿＿]
   ‾‾‾‾‾‾
    0.274

32) 3.548
   − [＿＿]
   ‾‾‾‾‾‾
    1.366

1)
$$2.351 - \boxed{} = 0.071$$

2)
$$2.718 - \boxed{} = 0.819$$

3)
$$4.077 - \boxed{} = 0.620$$

4)
$$3.486 - \boxed{} = 3.160$$

5)
$$2.136 - \boxed{} = 0.469$$

6)
$$2.394 - \boxed{} = 0.935$$

7)
$$3.290 - \boxed{} = 2.257$$

8)
$$3.605 - \boxed{} = 0.406$$

9)
$$3.129 - \boxed{} = 1.383$$

10)
$$2.028 - \boxed{} = 0.058$$

11)
$$4.613 - \boxed{} = 4.588$$

12)
$$3.759 - \boxed{} = 0.995$$

13)
$$2.790 - \boxed{} = 1.222$$

14)
$$1.889 - \boxed{} = 0.322$$

15)
$$4.101 - \boxed{} = 2.819$$

16)
$$4.788 - \boxed{} = 3.801$$

17)
$$4.456 - \boxed{} = 1.414$$

18)
$$3.385 - \boxed{} = 0.511$$

19)
$$1.436 - \boxed{} = 0.701$$

20)
$$2.337 - \boxed{} = 1.755$$

21)
$$4.656 - \boxed{} = 4.519$$

22)
$$4.406 - \boxed{} = 1.645$$

23)
$$4.286 - \boxed{} = 2.257$$

24)
$$4.245 - \boxed{} = 0.415$$

25)
$$3.676 - \boxed{} = 0.586$$

26)
$$1.047 - \boxed{} = 0.857$$

27)
$$4.119 - \boxed{} = 0.676$$

28)
$$3.761 - \boxed{} = 2.691$$

29)
$$4.050 - \boxed{} = 1.339$$

30)
$$2.151 - \boxed{} = 0.311$$

31)
$$3.495 - \boxed{} = 0.953$$

32)
$$4.861 - \boxed{} = 4.483$$

Level 11

Decimals

Multiplying decimals by decimals

1) 0.6
  × 0.2
  _____

2) 3.2
  × 3.9
  _____

3) 4.0
  × 1.6
  _____

4) 3.2
  × 0.6
  _____

5) 1.4
  × 2.5
  _____

6) 0.2
  × 3.8
  _____

7) 0.2
  × 2.7
  _____

8) 3.7
  × 1.1
  _____

9) 3.7
  × 3.0
  _____

10) 0.9
  × 1.5
  _____

11) 4.6
  × 0.4
  _____

12) 3.5
  × 2.5
  _____

13) 2.7
  × 2.9
  _____

14) 0.7
  × 0.4
  _____

15) 1.5
  × 0.7
  _____

16) 2.3
  × 2.0
  _____

17) 4.8
  × 3.0
  _____

18) 0.6
  × 0.6
  _____

19) 3.9
  × 1.4
  _____

20) 4.2
  × 1.9
  _____

21) 4.2
  × 0.5
  _____

22) 0.3
  × 0.1
  _____

23) 4.1
  × 3.0
  _____

24) 2.0
  × 3.1
  _____

25) 2.8
  × 2.3
  _____

26) 0.9
  × 1.0
  _____

27) 4.3
  × 1.1
  _____

28) 0.5
  × 3.4
  _____

29) 1.5
  × 0.9
  _____

30) 2.1
  × 0.3
  _____

31) 3.1
  × 3.8
  _____

32) 3.1
  × 2.6
  _____

33) 1.6
  × 0.9
  _____

34) 1.5
  × 0.4
  _____

35) 4.1
  × 2.9
  _____

36) 2.3
  × 2.5
  _____

37) 1.1
  × 1.8
  _____

38) 0.6
  × 2.2
  _____

39) 2.3
  × 0.9
  _____

40) 2.1
  × 0.3
  _____

1)
```
    3.7
×   3.4
──────
```

2)
```
    0.8
×   1.6
──────
```

3)
```
    4.4
×   2.2
──────
```

4)
```
    3.5
×   2.5
──────
```

5)
```
    3.7
×   2.7
──────
```

6)
```
    4.8
×   2.2
──────
```

7)
```
    2.8
×   0.7
──────
```

8)
```
    4.5
×   1.6
──────
```

9)
```
    1.7
×   2.2
──────
```

10)
```
    1.3
×   2.6
──────
```

11)
```
    2.8
×   2.5
──────
```

12)
```
    4.2
×   3.6
──────
```

13)
```
    4.3
×   1.5
──────
```

14)
```
    3.6
×   2.0
──────
```

15)
```
    1.4
×   2.3
──────
```

16)
```
    3.1
×   3.5
──────
```

17)
```
    3.7
×   1.4
──────
```

18)
```
    2.0
×   3.3
──────
```

19)
```
    2.6
×   1.1
──────
```

20)
```
    3.3
×   3.5
──────
```

21)
```
    3.8
×   4.0
──────
```

22)
```
    1.1
×   3.7
──────
```

23)
```
    0.4
×   1.7
──────
```

24)
```
    3.5
×   1.0
──────
```

25)
```
    3.1
×   0.5
──────
```

26)
```
    4.4
×   3.1
──────
```

27)
```
    0.9
×   2.5
──────
```

28)
```
    0.8
×   3.6
──────
```

29)
```
    0.5
×   3.6
──────
```

30)
```
    3.7
×   3.5
──────
```

31)
```
    3.7
×   2.5
──────
```

32)
```
    3.4
×   2.5
──────
```

33)
```
    3.6
×   2.1
──────
```

34)
```
    1.8
×   0.5
──────
```

35)
```
    2.3
×   0.7
──────
```

36)
```
    4.6
×   2.9
──────
```

37)
```
    1.0
×   2.2
──────
```

38)
```
    1.2
×   1.6
──────
```

39)
```
    3.7
×   0.1
──────
```

40)
```
    2.6
×   0.5
──────
```

1)   1.0
 × 1.1

2)   0.6
 × 3.6

3)   3.4
 × 3.2

4)   2.0
 × 0.8

5)   3.6
 × 1.8

6)   4.9
 × 1.9

7)   4.0
 × 3.3

8)   1.8
 × 1.3

9)   4.1
 × 2.3

10)   3.9
 × 3.6

11)   2.1
 × 1.7

12)   4.1
 × 3.7

13)   2.8
 × 0.2

14)   0.7
 × 2.1

15)   0.2
 × 2.9

16)   2.0
 × 0.3

17)   1.7
 × 1.0

18)   4.6
 × 2.6

19)   2.6
 × 1.1

20)   4.9
 × 3.7

21)   1.0
 × 1.4

22)   2.8
 × 2.6

23)   0.6
 × 0.6

24)   2.1
 × 0.2

25)   2.0
 × 0.8

26)   2.9
 × 0.6

27)   0.6
 × 2.6

28)   3.5
 × 2.3

29)   1.6
 × 0.6

30)   1.7
 × 0.7

31)   3.3
 × 1.9

32)   3.0
 × 3.3

33)   2.2
 × 3.2

34)   4.6
 × 1.0

35)   3.5
 × 2.8

36)   1.3
 × 2.9

37)   3.2
 × 3.3

38)   4.8
 × 1.8

39)   0.4
 × 1.2

40)   0.2
 × 3.8

1) 4.0
  × 0.8

2) 2.0
  × 2.7

3) 5.0
  × 3.5

4) 2.5
  × 2.6

5) 4.8
  × 0.9

6) 4.9
  × 0.1

7) 3.1
  × 1.3

8) 0.8
  × 2.4

9) 4.5
  × 1.6

10) 1.0
  × 3.4

11) 1.9
  × 2.6

12) 2.1
  × 2.0

13) 4.3
  × 0.8

14) 3.5
  × 1.6

15) 4.9
  × 1.9

16) 3.3
  × 3.0

17) 2.2
  × 2.9

18) 1.5
  × 3.9

19) 2.9
  × 3.0

20) 0.6
  × 2.1

21) 2.8
  × 1.6

22) 4.2
  × 2.2

23) 0.1
  × 1.5

24) 3.4
  × 1.0

25) 1.6
  × 2.2

26) 2.8
  × 3.7

27) 3.2
  × 2.0

28) 4.4
  × 2.9

29) 3.4
  × 1.7

30) 3.5
  × 0.3

31) 0.4
  × 1.5

32) 4.7
  × 3.6

33) 2.6
  × 0.7

34) 0.3
  × 0.1

35) 3.7
  × 2.4

36) 4.2
  × 0.2

37) 0.5
  × 3.4

38) 1.7
  × 1.2

39) 1.8
  × 3.8

40) 4.8
  × 1.3

1) 0.4
  × 3.1

2) 2.7
  × 3.2

3) 4.2
  × 3.6

4) 3.2
  × 2.0

5) 1.9
  × 3.3

6) 2.9
  × 1.1

7) 3.5
  × 1.2

8) 2.1
  × 2.5

9) 3.4
  × 2.2

10) 2.1
   × 0.2

11) 1.9
   × 3.6

12) 1.9
   × 3.5

13) 0.8
   × 2.2

14) 0.4
   × 3.1

15) 3.4
   × 4.0

16) 4.0
   × 2.5

17) 4.7
   × 2.7

18) 1.2
   × 1.7

19) 2.2
   × 3.3

20) 0.6
   × 3.8

21) 1.6
   × 3.2

22) 2.9
   × 2.4

23) 3.9
   × 2.9

24) 3.3
   × 2.8

25) 0.6
   × 3.9

26) 1.8
   × 0.6

27) 4.4
   × 2.2

28) 1.7
   × 0.4

29) 0.6
   × 0.1

30) 1.5
   × 3.2

31) 0.9
   × 1.5

32) 3.6
   × 1.9

33) 3.2
   × 2.5

34) 1.7
   × 0.9

35) 3.8
   × 2.2

36) 0.4
   × 3.7

37) 2.3
   × 1.6

38) 2.3
   × 3.1

39) 0.2
   × 3.6

40) 2.3
   × 1.2

1)
```
    1.1
×   2.4
─────
```

2)
```
    0.2
×   2.4
─────
```

3)
```
    2.7
×   0.7
─────
```

4)
```
    0.1
×   0.5
─────
```

5)
```
    0.5
×   0.7
─────
```

6)
```
    2.9
×   1.2
─────
```

7)
```
    4.4
×   3.9
─────
```

8)
```
    3.1
×   2.5
─────
```

9)
```
    1.6
×   1.4
─────
```

10)
```
    3.9
×   3.6
─────
```

11)
```
    4.9
×   1.6
─────
```

12)
```
    3.4
×   1.9
─────
```

13)
```
    2.5
×   1.7
─────
```

14)
```
    3.2
×   3.5
─────
```

15)
```
    3.9
×   1.4
─────
```

16)
```
    3.4
×   2.2
─────
```

17)
```
    0.1
×   2.6
─────
```

18)
```
    4.4
×   1.1
─────
```

19)
```
    0.5
×   3.4
─────
```

20)
```
    2.9
×   0.8
─────
```

21)
```
    4.0
×   1.2
─────
```

22)
```
    3.0
×   3.0
─────
```

23)
```
    1.9
×   1.4
─────
```

24)
```
    2.2
×   3.2
─────
```

25)
```
    2.1
×   1.9
─────
```

26)
```
    1.8
×   3.1
─────
```

27)
```
    2.5
×   0.8
─────
```

28)
```
    0.1
×   3.9
─────
```

29)
```
    0.5
×   1.9
─────
```

30)
```
    4.7
×   1.6
─────
```

31)
```
    2.1
×   2.1
─────
```

32)
```
    2.4
×   2.5
─────
```

33)
```
    4.0
×   0.5
─────
```

34)
```
    3.2
×   1.6
─────
```

35)
```
    1.4
×   1.8
─────
```

36)
```
    0.6
×   3.2
─────
```

37)
```
    1.9
×   3.3
─────
```

38)
```
    1.3
×   0.5
─────
```

39)
```
    4.1
×   1.3
─────
```

40)
```
    3.6
×   0.2
─────
```

Level 12

Decimals

Dividing decimals by decimals

1) 3.3 ÷ 0.4 = ☐

2) 0.4 ÷ 0.6 = ☐

3) 3.6 ÷ 2.2 = ☐

4) 0.4 ÷ 1.8 = ☐

5) 0.2 ÷ 0.1 = ☐

6) 2.9 ÷ 0.1 = ☐

7) 3.0 ÷ 0.6 = ☐

8) 2.7 ÷ 2.8 = ☐

9) 0.2 ÷ 3.1 = ☐

10) 2.0 ÷ 3.8 = ☐

11) 3.6 ÷ 1.9 = ☐

12) 4.5 ÷ 2.1 = ☐

13) 0.9 ÷ 0.9 = ☐

14) 0.3 ÷ 2.4 = ☐

15) 2.9 ÷ 2.0 = ☐

16) 0.7 ÷ 1.9 = ☐

17) 3.8 ÷ 2.6 = ☐

18) 3.6 ÷ 3.7 = ☐

19) 3.2 ÷ 0.4 = ☐

20) 2.5 ÷ 3.9 = ☐

21) 0.7 ÷ 3.3 = ☐

22) 4.0 ÷ 2.6 = ☐

23) 4.7 ÷ 2.8 = ☐

24) 4.4 ÷ 3.8 = ☐

25) 4.5 ÷ 3.8 = ☐

26) 3.0 ÷ 1.4 = ☐

27) 2.7 ÷ 1.4 = ☐

28) 1.9 ÷ 4.0 = ☐

29) 0.5 ÷ 3.2 = ☐

30) 1.1 ÷ 2.6 = ☐

31) 3.9 ÷ 0.6 = ☐

32) 1.7 ÷ 4.0 = ☐

33) 4.4 ÷ 1.4 = ☐

34) 2.4 ÷ 3.7 = ☐

35) 3.4 ÷ 2.5 = ☐

36) 0.6 ÷ 0.4 = ☐

37) 3.1 ÷ 0.7 = ☐

38) 2.3 ÷ 1.2 = ☐

39) 4.0 ÷ 0.5 = ☐

40) 3.1 ÷ 3.7 = ☐

1) $4.2 \div 2.6$

2) $3.0 \div 2.6$

3) $3.3 \div 3.1$

4) $1.8 \div 0.7$

5) $0.9 \div 2.4$

6) $4.5 \div 3.1$

7) $2.0 \div 2.8$

8) $1.6 \div 1.0$

9) $3.5 \div 3.5$

10) $3.1 \div 0.7$

11) $4.7 \div 2.6$

12) $4.2 \div 1.9$

13) $2.8 \div 3.4$

14) $4.1 \div 3.2$

15) $4.6 \div 3.0$

16) $4.2 \div 0.4$

17) $3.4 \div 3.5$

18) $0.8 \div 1.0$

19) $0.3 \div 2.6$

20) $1.1 \div 0.4$

21) $2.8 \div 3.8$

22) $4.7 \div 1.2$

23) $4.9 \div 0.8$

24) $4.0 \div 4.0$

25) $4.8 \div 0.8$

26) $4.0 \div 0.1$

27) $2.7 \div 3.9$

28) $1.0 \div 3.5$

29) $4.5 \div 0.3$

30) $0 \div 0$

31) $4.0 \div 0.4$

32) $4.6 \div 1.9$

33) $3.2 \div 1.8$

34) $2.4 \div 1.3$

35) $4.9 \div 0.5$

36) $3.8 \div 2.9$

37) $1.5 \div 1.1$

38) $2.8 \div 1.4$

39) $3.7 \div 0.8$

40) $5.0 \div 3.0$

1) 4.6 ÷ 0.9

2) 2.2 ÷ 3.2

3) 0.9 ÷ 1.6

4) 1.2 ÷ 3.3

5) 1.1 ÷ 2.6

6) 0.5 ÷ 3.8

7) 3.0 ÷ 3.2

8) 2.8 ÷ 3.1

9) 2.6 ÷ 2.8

10) 2.9 ÷ 0.4

11) 4.7 ÷ 0.4

12) 0.6 ÷ 3.9

13) 1.1 ÷ 3.8

14) 0.7 ÷ 1.3

15) 3.9 ÷ 2.5

16) 0.2 ÷ 1.2

17) 1.7 ÷ 3.4

18) 1.1 ÷ 0.0

19) 3.0 ÷ 2.5

20) 0.9 ÷ 3.3

21) 1.1 ÷ 3.1

22) 4.8 ÷ 3.7

23) 1.6 ÷ 0.2

24) 1.6 ÷ 3.8

25) 1.1 ÷ 1.3

26) 3.2 ÷ 2.7

27) 1.4 ÷ 2.7

28) 1.8 ÷ 1.3

29) 2.9 ÷ 1.0

30) 0.5 ÷ 0.2

31) 3.6 ÷ 0.7

32) 1.7 ÷ 0.9

33) 3.5 ÷ 0.2

34) 4.7 ÷ 2.7

35) 1.6 ÷ 0.7

36) 0.8 ÷ 2.7

37) 1.2 ÷ 3.4

38) 3.8 ÷ 3.0

39) 0.9 ÷ 2.2

40) 2.6 ÷ 1.0

1) 1.6 ÷ 1.9 ☐

2) 2.5 ÷ 3.7 ☐

3) 0.9 ÷ 0.3 ☐

4) 3.3 ÷ 2.1 ☐

5) 4.2 ÷ 0.8 ☐

6) 1.0 ÷ 1.1 ☐

7) 4.3 ÷ 1.3 ☐

8) 2.4 ÷ 0.2 ☐

9) 4.0 ÷ 2.3 ☐

10) 4.3 ÷ 1.5 ☐

11) 1.0 ÷ 1.9 ☐

12) 3.4 ÷ 3.5 ☐

13) 1.5 ÷ 0.0 ☐

14) 1.6 ÷ 0.2 ☐

15) 4.0 ÷ 2.9 ☐

16) 2.9 ÷ 1.3 ☐

17) 4.4 ÷ 1.8 ☐

18) 2.7 ÷ 0.7 ☐

19) 2.9 ÷ 2.0 ☐

20) 2.5 ÷ 4.0 ☐

21) 4.3 ÷ 3.9 ☐

22) 2.3 ÷ 2.0 ☐

23) 4.2 ÷ 1.7 ☐

24) 1.8 ÷ 2.0 ☐

25) 4.0 ÷ 1.2 ☐

26) 4.2 ÷ 2.8 ☐

27) 3.9 ÷ 3.2 ☐

28) 1.5 ÷ 1.3 ☐

29) 2.6 ÷ 2.8 ☐

30) 4.9 ÷ 2.6 ☐

31) 1.5 ÷ 1.6 ☐

32) 3.4 ÷ 2.5 ☐

33) 4.0 ÷ 1.1 ☐

34) 4.5 ÷ 2.1 ☐

35) 4.8 ÷ 3.7 ☐

36) 3.7 ÷ 3.4 ☐

37) 0.3 ÷ 3.4 ☐

38) 2.1 ÷ 4.0 ☐

39) 2.8 ÷ 0.8 ☐

40) 2.0 ÷ 2.0 ☐

1) 0.4 ÷ 2.6

2) 1.3 ÷ 2.2

3) 1.7 ÷ 0.6

4) 4.8 ÷ 2.2

5) 0.9 ÷ 1.7

6) 2.8 ÷ 3.2

7) 4.4 ÷ 3.2

8) 3.6 ÷ 2.8

9) 4.5 ÷ 1.8

10) 2.1 ÷ 0.3

11) 0.3 ÷ 1.9

12) 3.0 ÷ 3.6

13) 3.2 ÷ 3.0

14) 0.3 ÷ 2.2

15) 0.9 ÷ 1.3

16) 4.7 ÷ 2.3

17) 1.0 ÷ 2.3

18) 1.6 ÷ 1.9

19) 0.9 ÷ 3.9

20) 4.8 ÷ 2.9

21) 2.5 ÷ 0.4

22) 3.4 ÷ 1.2

23) 4.0 ÷ 4.0

24) 2.6 ÷ 1.7

25) 4.6 ÷ 3.8

26) 1.9 ÷ 1.7

27) 1.1 ÷ 1.0

28) 3.5 ÷ 3.2

29) 2.4 ÷ 1.2

30) 4.7 ÷ 2.2

31) 4.9 ÷ 3.2

32) 4.0 ÷ 2.7

33) 3.3 ÷ 1.1

34) 1.3 ÷ 1.8

35) 2.1 ÷ 0.8

36) 4.0 ÷ 4.0

37) 3.8 ÷ 0.1

38) 4.9 ÷ 0.5

39) 1.8 ÷ 3.6

40) 4.9 ÷ 3.6

1) 3.5 ÷ 0.9	2) 3.6 ÷ 3.8	3) 4.1 ÷ 2.0	4) 3.9 ÷ 2.0	5) 2.0 ÷ 3.2
6) 1.5 ÷ 2.9	7) 1.9 ÷ 0.5	8) 0.2 ÷ 2.0	9) 0.2 ÷ 1.7	10) 3.8 ÷ 2.1
11) 0.1 ÷ 0.6	12) 4.2 ÷ 1.3	13) 0.6 ÷ 0.8	14) 3.7 ÷ 0.4	15) 2.1 ÷ 0.1
16) 2.9 ÷ 2.5	17) 4.6 ÷ 3.8	18) 4.8 ÷ 2.3	19) 2.6 ÷ 2.3	20) 2.9 ÷ 3.8
21) 0.8 ÷ 2.6	22) 2.6 ÷ 3.0	23) 4.3 ÷ 3.6	24) 4.4 ÷ 1.1	25) 2.3 ÷ 3.4
26) 0.3 ÷ 0.4	27) 3.7 ÷ 0.2	28) 2.9 ÷ 1.3	29) 0.6 ÷ 0.5	30) 2.9 ÷ 1.7
31) 0.4 ÷ 1.0	32) 1.5 ÷ 2.2	33) 3.4 ÷ 1.1	34) 0.9 ÷ 1.9	35) 3.3 ÷ 1.8
36) 0.6 ÷ 1.2	37) 2.4 ÷ 3.1	38) 2.4 ÷ 3.9	39) 1.3 ÷ 3.7	40) 3.5 ÷ 2.6

Other math workbooks for your gifted 5th grader...

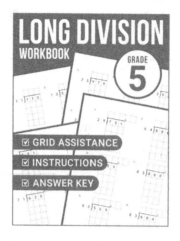

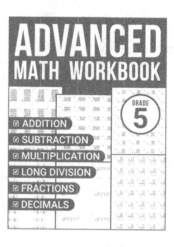

Scan the QR code below:

Scan the QR code below:

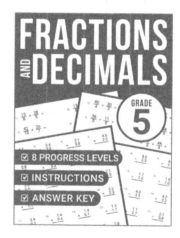

Scan the QR code below:

Scan the QR code below:

www.Nermilio.com

Answer Key

Page 8, Item 1:
(1)3531 (2)6419 (3)2249 (4)5140 (5)9482
(6)9169 (7)3709 (8)9577 (9)8177 (10)7533
(11)1860 (12)2362 (13)7434 (14)2618
(15)2241 (16)8009 (17)1852 (18)8660
(19)7810 (20)3159 (21)2578 (22)2189
(23)9332 (24)2432 (25)5147 (26)6408
(27)6220 (28)8810 (29)4526 (30)3239
(31)5402 (32)3373

Page 9, Item 1:
(1)7298 (2)7740 (3)6646 (4)5552 (5)7119
(6)9360 (7)9913 (8)6925 (9)3734 (10)6925
(11)1663 (12)5442 (13)8725 (14)8813
(15)5540 (16)8860 (17)6316 (18)6999
(19)4063 (20)7631 (21)9099 (22)7932
(23)4093 (24)1520 (25)6148 (26)5803
(27)5991 (28)3035 (29)1351 (30)8236
(31)8612 (32)2553

Page 10, Item 1:
(1)1897 (2)6754 (3)8063 (4)4510 (5)7357
(6)9708 (7)4063 (8)5854 (9)5777 (10)9149
(11)4805 (12)3148 (13)8343 (14)6020
(15)8978 (16)6762 (17)1450 (18)7519
(19)9376 (20)7472 (21)8558 (22)7293
(23)2055 (24)9722 (25)7236 (26)5020
(27)6141 (28)6705 (29)3939 (30)3264
(31)9924 (32)2084

Page 11, Item 1:
(1)1401 (2)6112 (3)6466 (4)9716 (5)6970
(6)1955 (7)1117 (8)2228 (9)4649 (10)4920
(11)8073 (12)3091 (13)3899 (14)1994
(15)3386 (16)6611 (17)3611 (18)3497
(19)6621 (20)6073 (21)8585 (22)7983
(23)2117 (24)2502 (25)8172 (26)8762
(27)2223 (28)1177 (29)9599 (30)7287
(31)8030 (32)5180

Page 12, Item 1:
(1)4501 (2)8731 (3)5950 (4)6851 (5)7162
(6)6400 (7)7056 (8)9325 (9)1129 (10)1541
(11)1151 (12)7735 (13)9472 (14)1356

(15)2912 (16)9475 (17)7153 (18)9805
(19)8890 (20)9427 (21)8829 (22)6101
(23)4848 (24)8817 (25)9691 (26)3403
(27)8799 (28)8206 (29)1733 (30)4520
(31)8139 (32)6566

Page 13, Item 1:
(1)7248 (2)1722 (3)5755 (4)7210 (5)3116
(6)7207 (7)1535 (8)1571 (9)7009 (10)4337
(11)9412 (12)5884 (13)7013 (14)8285
(15)6533 (16)3838 (17)2048 (18)8357
(19)6821 (20)2003 (21)7175 (22)6527
(23)7156 (24)8712 (25)1620 (26)4484
(27)9988 (28)1028 (29)1520 (30)9565
(31)2935 (32)7932

Page 14, Item 1:
(1)3395 (2)2989 (3)2469 (4)6198 (5)9787
(6)6159 (7)8630 (8)8944 (9)7784 (10)5845
(11)1130 (12)8361 (13)8269 (14)6005
(15)1327 (16)9059 (17)1402 (18)2314
(19)4253 (20)1686 (21)7501 (22)4374
(23)9293 (24)4951 (25)2810 (26)7122
(27)3981 (28)7640 (29)8834 (30)7361
(31)4109 (32)3829

Page 16, Item 1:
(1)7300 (2)5756 (3)2833 (4)5961 (5)1822
(6)1547 (7)2752 (8)2348 (9)2047 (10)5320
(11)3523 (12)6700 (13)6375 (14)2716
(15)3068 (16)1342 (17)2964 (18)3458
(19)1283 (20)1876 (21)2920 (22)2296
(23)3514 (24)4093 (25)4094 (26)2188
(27)1780 (28)5707 (29)5689 (30)4767
(31)2070 (32)3552

Page 17, Item 1:
(1)2813 (2)1573 (3)6389 (4)6860 (5)2664
(6)4826 (7)3600 (8)4307 (9)1871 (10)3970
(11)5843 (12)2707 (13)3182 (14)8327
(15)9076 (16)4202 (17)6642 (18)4987
(19)1252 (20)4651 (21)5787 (22)6580
(23)6657 (24)7197 (25)1132 (26)1442
(27)3749 (28)3564 (29)4331 (30)5693
(31)1182 (32)3873
Page 18, Item 1:
(1)4113 (2)5051 (3)1700 (4)2558 (5)6911
(6)1136 (7)7575 (8)3851 (9)1908 (10)2099
(11)1574 (12)1761 (13)5191 (14)5604
(15)1657 (16)5360 (17)2542 (18)2730
(19)8555 (20)1061 (21)2313 (22)4852
(23)5527 (24)4971 (25)2119 (26)3575
(27)4066 (28)8455 (29)1720 (30)2336
(31)6022 (32)1262
Page 19, Item 1:
(1)1629 (2)3552 (3)2075 (4)3829 (5)2103
(6)3655 (7)3185 (8)9041 (9)1501 (10)4913
(11)6405 (12)7282 (13)4552 (14)4774
(15)2363 (16)6533 (17)5752 (18)2187
(19)1644 (20)3809 (21)4572 (22)1217
(23)1868 (24)3865 (25)3867 (26)4471
(27)6362 (28)4776 (29)1382 (30)4050
(31)1158 (32)1061
Page 20, Item 1:
(1)3275 (2)8690 (3)3103 (4)5059 (5)6011
(6)4264 (7)7304 (8)2044 (9)2016 (10)6263
(11)1975 (12)1510 (13)3839 (14)2742
(15)1246 (16)2300 (17)3042 (18)3666
(19)4197 (20)3765 (21)1990 (22)3832
(23)1776 (24)6831 (25)1692 (26)1420
(27)4363 (28)3599 (29)7246 (30)6216
(31)1010 (32)3524
Page 21, Item 1:
(1)3602 (2)4411 (3)6128 (4)5487 (5)1475
(6)3070 (7)3646 (8)5359 (9)2726 (10)3649
(11)1672 (12)1407 (13)3035 (14)3874
(15)1336 (16)3070 (17)5451 (18)4291
(19)3846 (20)4957 (21)1140 (22)2404
(23)4236 (24)7699 (25)1067 (26)4108
(27)3723 (28)2151 (29)3820 (30)4542
(31)6489 (32)5928
Page 22, Item 1:
(1)4355 (2)3707 (3)1431 (4)5187 (5)6852
(6)4158 (7)2432 (8)1510 (9)1319 (10)5955
(11)2703 (12)3296 (13)2669 (14)4433
(15)2579 (16)3126 (17)2190 (18)3951
(19)2005 (20)2034 (21)1074 (22)1763
(23)6012 (24)1886 (25)3052 (26)6231
(27)2261 (28)3658 (29)1146 (30)1968
(31)3522 (32)8086
Page 24, Item 1:
(1)58310 (2)301223 (3)247404 (4)610234
(5)303555 (6)218694 (7)109737 (8)331378
(9)27499 (10)474250 (11)158368
(12)568727 (13)758880 (14)342300
(15)127100 (16)106974 (17)30174
(18)566262 (19)450468 (20)131733
(21)414276 (22)57570 (23)499746
(24)782278 (25)109989 (26)490432
(27)76744 (28)127332 (29)145111
(30)39576 (31)172800 (32)305890
Page 25, Item 1:
(1)178200 (2)41760 (3)182970 (4)344705
(5)132544 (6)97206 (7)326781 (8)753303
(9)330998 (10)503424 (11)375875
(12)206127 (13)330072 (14)269679
(15)716680 (16)335040 (17)316078

(18)453000 (19)282416 (20)423591
(21)462800 (22)147702 (23)15194
(24)308700 (25)287206 (26)188106
(27)453067 (28)237650 (29)186900
(30)239364 (31)285645 (32)736524

Page 26, Item 1:

(1)225105 (2)116900 (3)294816 (4)96432
(5)216942 (6)563328 (7)510300 (8)112497
(9)423192 (10)397460 (11)695552
(12)285552 (13)437152 (14)196947
(15)711375 (16)506880 (17)271834
(18)201536 (19)247929 (20)475308
(21)864500 (22)82840 (23)109212
(24)60962 (25)92852 (26)394450
(27)609765 (28)120540 (29)360525
(30)122512 (31)233946 (32)387360

Page 27, Item 1:

(1)344955 (2)763875 (3)155040 (4)62677
(5)91080 (6)46336 (7)279500 (8)842363
(9)321135 (10)144320 (11)455715
(12)101840 (13)284809 (14)133035
(15)138992 (16)169320 (17)348952
(18)171700 (19)78490 (20)379424
(21)123900 (22)103212 (23)613110
(24)444876 (25)296744 (26)320465
(27)257040 (28)647808 (29)87750
(30)108108 (31)82264 (32)30856

Page 28, Item 1:

(1)853794 (2)128790 (3)61985 (4)367563
(5)130803 (6)725208 (7)176351 (8)135415
(9)269460 (10)346104 (11)530671
(12)27360 (13)98832 (14)282072
(15)207507 (16)128520 (17)418432
(18)799220 (19)167808 (20)30927
(21)871921 (22)78390 (23)224504
(24)145160 (25)824502 (26)900564
(27)202101 (28)75495 (29)143313
(30)533832 (31)145317 (32)134832

Page 29, Item 1:

(1)217338 (2)152000 (3)68445 (4)306364

(5)107996 (6)196245 (7)690795 (8)113202
(9)293454 (10)724890 (11)137562
(12)392466 (13)735286 (14)456705
(15)82818 (16)401676 (17)96360
(18)408915 (19)478936 (20)459136
(21)382151 (22)129259 (23)627228
(24)43337 (25)189426 (26)307755
(27)382184 (28)376464 (29)327699
(30)445764 (31)94240 (32)481328

Page 30, Item 1:

(1)98044 (2)193815 (3)63125 (4)500976
(5)613075 (6)81432 (7)312897 (8)435501
(9)328100 (10)401506 (11)118978
(12)256665 (13)850329 (14)289435
(15)499590 (16)396000 (17)345450
(18)333153 (19)96944 (20)271375
(21)52084 (22)38252 (23)212148
(24)51943 (25)175985 (26)200136
(27)76505 (28)157644 (29)102718
(30)808685 (31)786786 (32)81054

Page 32, Item 1:

(1)

```
              1 2 3 9 R2
      20)2 4 7 8 2
        - 2 0
          4 7
        -   4 0
            7 8
          -   6 0
              1 8 2
            - 1 8 0
                  2
```

(2)

```
              3 3 2 2 R8
      15)4 9 8 3 8
        - 4 5
          4 8
        - 4 5
            3 3
          - 3 0
              3 8
            - 3 0
                8
```

(7)

```
              9 4 1 R1 9
      48)4 5 1 8 7
        - 4 3 2
            1 9 8
          - 1 9 2
                6 7
              - 4 8
                1 9
```

(3)

```
              1 0 7 8 R3 6
      37)3 9 9 2 2
        - 3 7
          2 9
        -     0
          2 9 2
          - 2 5 9
              3 3 2
            - 2 9 6
                3 6
```

(8)

```
              5 1 0 R1 3
      41)2 0 9 2 3
        - 2 0 5
            4 2
          - 4 1
              1 3
            -   0
              1 3
```

Page 33, Item 1:

(4)

```
              2 1 8 0 R2 1
      23)5 0 1 6 1
        - 4 6
          4 1
        - 2 3
            1 8 6
          - 1 8 4
                2 1
              -   0
                2 1
```

(5)

```
              1 1 4 0 R3 4
      42)4 7 9 1 4
        - 4 2
          5 9
        - 4 2
            1 7 1
          - 1 6 8
                3 4
              -   0
                3 4
```

(6)

```
              2 2 2 0 R2 4
      43)9 5 4 8 4
        - 8 6
          9 4
        - 8 6
            8 8
          - 8 6
              2 4
            -   0
              2 4
```

Page 99

(1)
```
        2 2 4 3 R1
  1 9 ) 4 2 6 1 8
      - 3 8
        4 6
      - 3 8
          8 1
        - 7 6
            5 8
          - 5 7
              1
```

(2)
```
        3 5 4 6 R1
  1 4 ) 4 9 6 4 5
      - 4 2
        7 6
      - 7 0
          6 4
        - 5 6
            8 5
          - 8 4
              1
```

(7)
```
          7 9 6 R1
  3 4 ) 2 7 0 6 5
      - 2 3 8
          3 2 6
        - 3 0 6
            2 0 5
          - 2 0 4
                1
```

(8)
```
        1 7 8 9 R8
  4 2 ) 7 5 1 4 6
      - 4 2
        3 3 1
      - 2 9 4
          3 7 4
        - 3 3 6
            3 8 6
          - 3 7 8
                8
```

(3)
```
        5 3 7 R1 2
  2 4 ) 1 2 9 0 0
      - 1 2 0
            9 0
          - 7 2
            1 8 0
          - 1 6 8
              1 2
```

Page 34, Item 1:

(1)
```
        2 3 2 7 R2 0
  3 3 ) 7 6 8 1 1
      - 6 6
        1 0 8
      -   9 9
            9 1
          - 6 6
            2 5 1
          - 2 3 1
              2 0
```

(4)
```
        5 6 2 5 R1 2
  1 5 ) 8 4 3 8 7
      - 7 5
        9 3
      - 9 0
          3 8
        - 3 0
            8 7
          - 7 5
            1 2
```

(2)
```
        2 0 1 9 R2 7
  4 2 ) 8 4 8 2 5
      - 8 4
        0 8
      -   0
          8 2
        - 4 2
          4 0 5
        - 3 7 8
            2 7
```

(5)
```
        1 9 2 7 R3 8
  4 1 ) 7 9 0 4 5
      - 4 1
        3 8 0
      - 3 6 9
          1 1 4
        -   8 2
            3 2 5
          - 2 8 7
              3 8
```

(6)
```
        2 0 0 1 R1 6
  1 9 ) 3 8 0 3 5
      - 3 8
        0 0
      -   0
          0 3
        -   0
            3 5
          - 1 9
            1 6
```

(3)
```
              2 0 2 5 R6
        ┌─────────────
    2 4 │ 4 8 6 0 6
        - 4 8
          ─────
            0 6
        -    0
          ─────
            6 0
          - 4 8
          ─────
            1 2 6
          - 1 2 0
          ───────
                6
```

(4)
```
              1 3 4 0 R2 2
        ┌─────────────
    4 6 │ 6 1 6 6 2
        - 4 6
          ─────
          1 5 6
        - 1 3 8
          ─────
            1 8 6
          - 1 8 4
          ───────
              2 2
          -    0
          ───────
              2 2
```

(5)
```
              1 2 7 6 R6
        ┌─────────────
    4 6 │ 5 8 7 0 2
        - 4 6
          ─────
          1 2 7
        -   9 2
          ─────
            3 5 0
          - 3 2 2
          ───────
              2 8 2
          -   2 7 6
          ───────
                6
```

(6)
```
              4 3 2 9 R9
        ┌─────────────
    1 8 │ 7 7 9 3 1
        - 7 2
          ─────
            5 9
          - 5 4
          ─────
            5 3
          - 3 6
          ─────
            1 7 1
          - 1 6 2
          ───────
                9
```

(7)
```
              6 7 6 R2 1
        ┌─────────────
    4 3 │ 2 9 0 8 9
        - 2 5 8
          ─────
            3 2 8
          - 3 0 1
          ───────
              2 7 9
          - 2 5 8
          ───────
              2 1
```

(8)
```
              7 8 6 R8
        ┌─────────────
    2 6 │ 2 0 4 4 4
        - 1 8 2
          ─────
            2 2 4
          - 2 0 8
          ───────
            1 6 4
          - 1 5 6
          ───────
                8
```

Page 35, Item 1:

(1)
```
              2 2 5 9 R1 1
        ┌─────────────
    4 0 │ 9 0 3 7 1
        - 8 0
          ─────
          1 0 3
        -   8 0
          ─────
            2 3 7
          - 2 0 0
          ───────
              3 7 1
          - 3 6 0
          ───────
                1 1
```

(2)
```
              1 1 7 6 R4
        ┌─────────────
    4 8 │ 5 6 4 5 2
        - 4 8
          ─────
            8 4
          - 4 8
          ─────
            3 6 5
          - 3 3 6
          ───────
              2 9 2
          - 2 8 8
          ───────
                4
```

(3)
```
              2 3 1 1 R1
        ┌─────────────
    2 3 │ 5 3 1 5 4
        - 4 6
          ─────
            7 1
          - 6 9
          ─────
            2 5
          - 2 3
          ─────
            2 4
          - 2 3
          ─────
              1
```

(4)
```
          6 2 7 R3
  2 9 ) 1 8 1 8 6
      - 1 7 4
          7 8
        - 5 8
          2 0 6
        - 2 0 3
              3
```

(5)
```
          3 0 0 3 R8
  2 8 ) 8 4 0 9 2
      - 8 4
          0 0
        -   0
            0 9
          -   0
              9 2
            - 8 4
                8
```

(2)
```
          2 1 6 9 R13
  3 9 ) 8 4 6 0 4
      - 7 8
          6 6
        - 3 9
          2 7 0
        - 2 3 4
            3 6 4
          - 3 5 1
              1 3
```

(6)
```
          1 2 5 6 R17
  3 0 ) 3 7 6 9 7
      - 3 0
          7 6
        - 6 0
          1 6 9
        - 1 5 0
            1 9 7
          - 1 8 0
              1 7
```

(3)
```
          2 2 1 8 R4
  4 5 ) 9 9 8 1 4
      - 9 0
          9 8
        - 9 0
            8 1
          - 4 5
            3 6 4
          - 3 6 0
                4
```

(7)
```
          6 7 7 R18
  2 9 ) 1 9 6 5 1
      - 1 7 4
          2 2 5
        - 2 0 3
            2 2 1
          - 2 0 3
              1 8
```

(4)
```
          2 0 2 5 R14
  3 2 ) 6 4 8 1 4
      - 6 4
          0 8
        -   0
            8 1
          - 6 4
            1 7 4
          - 1 6 0
              1 4
```

(8)
```
          7 8 4 R3
  1 3 ) 1 0 1 9 5
      -   9 1
          1 0 9
        - 1 0 4
              5 5
            - 5 2
                3
```

Page 36, Item 1:

(1)
```
          3 3 0 1 R19
  2 4 ) 7 9 2 4 3
      - 7 2
          7 2
        - 7 2
            0 4
          -   0
              4 3
            - 2 4
              1 9
```

Page 102

(5)
```
              6  9  6 R1 9
    2 6 ) 1  8  1  1  5
        - 1  5  6
              2  5  1
            - 2  3  4
                  1  7  5
                - 1  5  6
                      1  9
```

(2)
```
              4  5  7 R3 4
    4 1 ) 1  8  7  7  1
        - 1  6  4
              2  3  7
            - 2  0  5
                  3  2  1
                - 2  8  7
                      3  4
```

(6)
```
              7  9  8 R1 2
    3 5 ) 2  7  9  4  2
        - 2  4  5
              3  4  4
            - 3  1  5
                  2  9  2
                - 2  8  0
                      1  2
```

(3)
```
              6  6  0  6 R1 2
    1 4 ) 9  2  4  9  6
        - 8  4
              8  4
            - 8  4
                  0  9
                -    0
                      9  6
                    - 8  4
                          1  2
```

(7)
```
              3  4  2  6 R0
    2 2 ) 7  5  3  7  2
        - 6  6
              9  3
            - 8  8
                  5  7
                - 4  4
                      1  3  2
                    - 1  3  2
                            0
```

(4)
```
              5  7  6 R2 4
    4 5 ) 2  5  9  4  4
        - 2  2  5
              3  4  4
            - 3  1  5
                  2  9  4
                - 2  7  0
                      2  4
```

(8)
```
              8  2  6 R1 4
    1 5 ) 1  2  4  0  4
        - 1  2  0
              4  0
            - 3  0
                  1  0  4
                -    9  0
                      1  4
```

Page 37, Item 1:

(1)
```
              8  7  6 R4 2
    4 7 ) 4  1  2  1  4
        - 3  7  6
              3  6  1
            - 3  2  9
                  3  2  4
                - 2  8  2
                      4  2
```

(5)
```
            2 0 2 9 R1 2
    2 4 ) 4 8 7 0 8
        - 4 8
          0 7
        -   0
          7 0
        - 4 8
          2 2 8
        - 2 1 6
            1 2
```

(6)
```
            6 8 4 R6
    4 3 ) 2 9 4 1 8
        - 2 5 8
          3 6 1
        - 3 4 4
            1 7 8
        - 1 7 2
              6
```

(7)
```
            3 2 1 R1
    3 6 ) 1 1 5 5 7
        - 1 0 8
            7 5
        -   7 2
            3 7
        -   3 6
              1
```

(8)
```
            5 5 4 R1 5
    1 9 ) 1 0 5 4 1
        -   9 5
          1 0 4
        -   9 5
            9 1
        -   7 6
            1 5
```

Page 39, Item 1:
(1)5 151/187 (2)9 21/150 (3)2 522/840
(4)2 237/2009 (5)2 633/950 (6)2 583/1353
(7)2 825/1406 (8)3 297/325 (9)3 69/220
(10)11 7/92 (11)3 113/966 (12)2 726/1505
(13)4 20/198 (14)2 373/476 (15)3 334/731
(16)2 164/352 (17)2 375/1677 (18)3 2/84
(19)3 325/828 (20)4 185/510
Page 40, Item 1:
(1)5 251/273 (2)3 298/348 (3)3 247/777
(4)3 19/714 (5)3 253/400 (6)5 185/403
(7)3 330/861 (8)2 162/429 (9)2 179/275
(10)2 326/1568 (11)3 403/912
(12)3 274/532 (13)2 151/468 (14)3 34/900
(15)3 126/152 (16)3 37/299 (17)10 13/45
(18)2 311/1845 (19)3 119/520

(20)2 566/646
Page 41, Item 1:
(1)2 216/494 (2)3 4/132 (3)7 65/66
(4)2 303/700 (5)2 92/304 (6)3 36/546
(7)2 275/1470 (8)4 182/210 (9)2 770/1665
(10)2 300/1406 (11)2 183/238
(12)2 251/286 (13)3 213/435
(14)2 217/1110 (15)5 303/328
(16)2 162/725 (17)2 783/817 (18)3 266/697
(19)3 82/418 (20)4 21/75
Page 42, Item 1:
(1)2 304/644 (2)3 23/140 (3)2 103/840
(4)2 527/1161 (5)2 962/1519 (6)2 120/546
(7)4 54/144 (8)2 236/259 (9)2 447/1066
(10)3 121/725 (11)2 69/108 (12)2 595/950
(13)2 85/288 (14)2 878/1320 (15)2 552/900
(16)3 148/176 (17)3 438/702 (18)2 286/602
(19)3 94/330 (20)2 93/108
Page 43, Item 1:
(1)2 292/1426 (2)3 353/777 (3)2 508/1665
(4)5 45/230 (5)2 366/372 (6)2 110/172
(7)2 63/150 (8)5 21/104 (9)4 211/390
(10)9 69/145 (11)2 240/460 (12)3 77/216
(13)2 201/924 (14)2 10/96 (15)2 76/175
(16)10 128/205 (17)3 166/646
(18)2 440/627 (19)2 480/1517 (20)9 89/99
Page 44, Item 1:
(1)3 277/666 (2)5 110/312 (3)12 68/93
(4)2 867/1148 (5)2 6/42 (6)2 552/1155
(7)2 16/120 (8)2 369/1044 (9)2 650/805
(10)2 48/210 (11)2 327/855 (12)5 148/208
(13)3 4/48 (14)2 141/224 (15)2 46/90

(16)3 85/468 (17)5 150/304 (18)8 43/60
(19)4 206/238 (20)6 142/216

Page 46, Item 1:
(1)2 207/231 (2)9 42/140 (3)108/234
(4)9 38/52 (5)195/1189 (6)335/660
(7)4 50/104 (8)60/918 (9)285/1628
(10)50/165 (11)78/1120 (12)24/806
(13)171/1892 (14)45/182 (15)119/966
(16)91/1330 (17)11/45 (18)1 131/544
(19)1 438/855 (20)2 22/494

Page 47, Item 1:
(1)347/420 (2)121/756 (3)122/520
(4)250/1184 (5)8 136/195 (6)651/828
(7)1 190/493 (8)1 220/741 (9)254/408
(10)4 33/40 (11)288/672 (12)4 47/98
(13)494/1645 (14)262/525 (15)1 524/555
(16)6/42 (17)49/612 (18)1 110/238
(19)345/1406 (20)2 1/345

Page 48, Item 1:
(1)269/775 (2)29/1665 (3)1 35/210
(4)107/190 (5)2 131/156 (6)259/782
(7)10/297 (8)2 96/462 (9)249/1880
(10)130/506 (11)265/1421 (12)60/468
(13)24/108 (14)323/1092 (15)4 14/60
(16)3 23/30 (17)124/176 (18)307/713
(19)1 2/220 (20)4/506

Page 49, Item 1:
(1)2 33/228 (2)180/714 (3)2 59/297
(4)1 163/220 (5)2 54/228 (6)2/528
(7)1 43/120 (8)156/180 (9)14/798
(10)176/522 (11)4 171/220 (12)3 51/58
(13)5/2156 (14)4 70/136 (15)441/638
(16)241/1161 (17)529/1092 (18)115/126
(19)184/308 (20)1 2/28

Page 50, Item 1:
(1)149/168 (2)1 251/572 (3)3 44/69
(4)809/1035 (5)249/874 (6)260/1081
(7)103/209 (8)272/396 (9)35/1178
(10)7/390 (11)2 331/588 (12)1 186/624
(13)626/1504 (14)1 14/352 (15)16/60

(16)40/90 (17)348/798 (18)1 127/253
(19)42/480 (20)1 10/48

Page 51, Item 1:
(1)410/860 (2)3 11/224 (3)29/360
(4)320/594 (5)4 1/273 (6)2 11/30 (7)31/88
(8)36/680 (9)186/494 (10)421/459
(11)86/210 (12)94/1012 (13)202/323
(14)2 188/190 (15)978/1316 (16)30/432
(17)10 24/52 (18)23 9/38 (19)235/252
(20)1 17/90

Page 53, Item 1:
(1)12/56 (2)12/90 (3)24/84 (4)6/56 (5)6/84
(6)4/36 (7)4/48 (8)2/40 (9)3/24 (10)4/30
(11)2/55 (12)6/48 (13)5/24 (14)12/35
(15)2/36 (16)9/24 (17)2/8 (18)1/72
(19)15/24 (20)3/18 (21)12/72 (22)3/20
(23)2/8 (24)10/60 (25)10/120 (26)12/40
(27)18/88 (28)3/80 (29)6/30 (30)4/56

Page 54, Item 1:
(1)20/96 (2)56/132 (3)28/66 (4)14/54
(5)12/33 (6)20/72 (7)40/63 (8)8/54 (9)4/30
(10)24/40 (11)2/15 (12)5/12 (13)6/60
(14)2/24 (15)9/28 (16)3/14 (17)9/48
(18)10/21 (19)2/8 (20)5/40 (21)28/132
(22)2/21 (23)8/24 (24)9/44 (25)18/40
(26)5/44 (27)2/15 (28)7/72 (29)2/18
(30)35/96

Page 55, Item 1:
(1)3/16 (2)24/44 (3)2/21 (4)24/77 (5)18/48
(6)1/6 (7)6/16 (8)5/28 (9)1/45 (10)2/10
(11)2/20 (12)30/63 (13)2/10 (14)10/36

(15)9/72 (16)12/48 (17)6/120 (18)56/120
(19)14/48 (20)18/36 (21)1/24 (22)16/36
(23)3/54 (24)2/10 (25)14/33 (26)14/63
(27)6/14 (28)2/12 (29)10/120 (30)16/90

Page 56, Item 1:

(1)3/18 (2)18/55 (3)4/16 (4)6/54 (5)14/44
(6)8/99 (7)3/40 (8)5/99 (9)36/110
(10)28/90 (11)2/6 (12)4/33 (13)2/6
(14)16/55 (15)2/12 (16)16/45 (17)2/48
(18)5/20 (19)7/24 (20)4/21 (21)2/18
(22)14/60 (23)2/48 (24)4/33 (25)3/20
(26)4/56 (27)12/32 (28)4/35 (29)6/80
(30)10/90

Page 57, Item 1:

(1)4/60 (2)6/15 (3)16/120 (4)2/80 (5)30/44
(6)7/24 (7)9/120 (8)8/54 (9)6/15 (10)10/60
(11)9/40 (12)12/96 (13)16/132 (14)24/80
(15)1/44 (16)14/27 (17)1/20 (18)10/60
(19)35/70 (20)3/27 (21)10/132 (22)8/24
(23)3/8 (24)15/54 (25)4/72 (26)30/44
(27)15/60 (28)5/24 (29)8/33 (30)12/30

Page 58, Item 1:

(1)1/56 (2)1/14 (3)20/88 (4)6/84 (5)10/60
(6)28/99 (7)6/24 (8)3/8 (9)2/18 (10)6/36
(11)4/60 (12)15/90 (13)4/20 (14)28/45
(15)10/88 (16)9/84 (17)32/99 (18)3/24
(19)4/15 (20)12/77 (21)2/16 (22)6/48
(23)30/108 (24)1/20 (25)2/55 (26)30/84
(27)1/88 (28)1/33 (29)15/80 (30)6/44

Page 60, Item 1:

(1)24/20 (2)14/9 (3)30/36 (4)7/2 (5)72/10
(6)6/5 (7)24/21 (8)14/15 (9)10/8 (10)3/4
(11)14/18 (12)56/45 (13)27/8 (14)30/40
(15)7/2 (16)10/12 (17)4/5 (18)20/6
(19)35/16 (20)6/5 (21)27/36 (22)30/16
(23)8/9 (24)36/50 (25)5/16 (26)3/5
(27)12/8 (28)40/81 (29)45/6 (30)8/3

Page 61, Item 1:

(1)3/2 (2)6/5 (3)10/35 (4)20/9 (5)10/9
(6)24/20 (7)14/9 (8)10/8 (9)36/35 (10)6/15

(11)54/30 (12)10/3 (13)9/8 (14)18/10
(15)9/14 (16)36/40 (17)3/4 (18)2/6 (19)6/5
(20)30/54 (21)9/16 (22)20/6 (23)25/24
(24)24/16 (25)14/8 (26)5/6 (27)6/10
(28)25/7 (29)56/63 (30)35/20

Page 62, Item 1:

(1)36/28 (2)42/30 (3)8/14 (4)9/4 (5)10/8
(6)45/56 (7)25/8 (8)10/4 (9)20/12
(10)18/56 (11)45/49 (12)10/7 (13)10/12
(14)28/60 (15)24/28 (16)10/28 (17)5/6
(18)12/14 (19)70/48 (20)8/27 (21)40/15
(22)7/12 (23)15/32 (24)10/12 (25)6/10
(26)35/40 (27)30/49 (28)16/15 (29)40/45
(30)21/18

Page 63, Item 1:

(1)21/16 (2)2/10 (3)50/56 (4)20/56 (5)9/24
(6)60/36 (7)24/50 (8)45/49 (9)10/9
(10)40/9 (11)6/12 (12)6/5 (13)24/30
(14)2/8 (15)36/45 (16)12/10 (17)45/40
(18)10/32 (19)12/8 (20)9/18 (21)25/8
(22)10/6 (23)8/6 (24)8/9 (25)10/6 (26)10/9
(27)6/4 (28)14/8 (29)12/5 (30)40/35

Page 64, Item 1:

(1)5/2 (2)7/6 (3)5/3 (4)9/2 (5)5/6 (6)10/9
(7)60/9 (8)8/12 (9)5/12 (10)16/35
(11)20/18 (12)16/70 (13)7/12 (14)9/15
(15)10/48 (16)20/8 (17)8/6 (18)18/30
(19)6/16 (20)18/24 (21)32/18 (22)2/4
(23)10/12 (24)5/12 (25)7/2 (26)6/4 (27)8/6
(28)40/45 (29)9/14 (30)10/8

Page 65, Item 1:

(1)6/16 (2)10/12 (3)20/16 (4)10/6 (5)12/10
(6)9/6 (7)50/35 (8)24/40 (9)8/3 (10)30/35
(11)27/24 (12)9/25 (13)16/18 (14)3/6
(15)30/35 (16)8/54 (17)9/5 (18)40/64
(19)14/16 (20)12/30 (21)15/16 (22)8/20
(23)15/10 (24)2/5 (25)8/5 (26)49/16
(27)42/45 (28)8/3 (29)7/4 (30)9/12

Page 67, Item 1:

(1)2.326 (2)3.963 (3)2.560 (4)3.352
(5)1.109 (6)0.856 (7)2.588 (8)1.032
(9)4.984 (10)0.660 (11)0.323 (12)0.469
(13)0.945 (14)4.523 (15)3.031 (16)1.940
(17)3.659 (18)0.558 (19)3.188 (20)2.027
(21)1.984 (22)3.146 (23)3.548 (24)1.339
(25)1.061 (26)0.557 (27)4.714 (28)4.092
(29)1.707 (30)3.723 (31)0.365 (32)0.134

Page 68, Item 1:

(1)1.024 (2)3.471 (3)1.391 (4)4.009
(5)2.690 (6)4.707 (7)4.863 (8)4.600
(9)4.326 (10)2.802 (11)2.099 (12)2.285
(13)1.268 (14)4.310 (15)0.534 (16)2.064
(17)2.160 (18)2.198 (19)4.818 (20)2.260
(21)4.978 (22)3.025 (23)4.995 (24)1.005
(25)0.070 (26)2.881 (27)1.836 (28)2.487
(29)3.307 (30)1.069 (31)1.881 (32)3.882

Page 69, Item 1:

(1)2.587 (2)4.062 (3)1.635 (4)4.211
(5)0.574 (6)4.782 (7)2.778 (8)1.143
(9)1.570 (10)4.637 (11)3.876 (12)4.977
(13)3.768 (14)0.641 (15)4.511 (16)2.534
(17)2.320 (18)1.790 (19)1.388 (20)0.404
(21)0.806 (22)2.942 (23)3.187 (24)2.094
(25)0.085 (26)2.604 (27)2.605 (28)2.312
(29)2.102 (30)4.126 (31)2.809 (32)4.889

Page 70, Item 1:

(1)4.315 (2)3.399 (3)1.649 (4)2.682
(5)3.442 (6)0.844 (7)1.302 (8)1.492
(9)4.538 (10)0.656 (11)1.133 (12)2.223
(13)3.607 (14)2.633 (15)3.817 (16)0.096
(17)1.306 (18)1.633 (19)0.208 (20)2.567

(21)4.498 (22)2.147 (23)2.173 (24)4.664
(25)2.625 (26)2.326 (27)0.205 (28)4.219
(29)3.747 (30)3.425 (31)1.908 (32)0.905

Page 71, Item 1:

(1)2.547 (2)0.440 (3)1.542 (4)2.322
(5)0.398 (6)4.088 (7)0.801 (8)0.637
(9)2.399 (10)2.904 (11)3.825 (12)1.622
(13)1.771 (14)0.663 (15)3.230 (16)1.426
(17)4.318 (18)2.519 (19)3.404 (20)0.139
(21)4.066 (22)3.349 (23)1.188 (24)4.447
(25)4.483 (26)4.175 (27)2.906 (28)0.080
(29)4.339 (30)4.273 (31)4.133 (32)2.911

Page 72, Item 1:

(1)1.288 (2)4.562 (3)0.591 (4)0.360
(5)2.078 (6)1.410 (7)3.727 (8)3.323
(9)4.771 (10)0.322 (11)4.946 (12)1.602
(13)4.740 (14)1.701 (15)2.303 (16)0.623
(17)1.602 (18)0.972 (19)1.626 (20)4.072
(21)4.980 (22)2.434 (23)0.883 (24)1.463
(25)2.221 (26)0.938 (27)4.119 (28)0.608
(29)1.733 (30)1.976 (31)1.742 (32)1.164

Page 74, Item 1:

(1)0.681 (2)3.233 (3)0.668 (4)3.874
(5)0.583 (6)0.357 (7)3.196 (8)2.119
(9)0.188 (10)3.126 (11)1.861 (12)0.599
(13)3.216 (14)3.053 (15)2.505 (16)1.349
(17)2.096 (18)1.448 (19)2.905 (20)2.858
(21)2.266 (22)0.935 (23)0.635 (24)1.373
(25)2.606 (26)1.223 (27)2.144 (28)2.369
(29)1.447 (30)1.582 (31)2.603 (32)1.588

Page 75, Item 1:

(1)1.497 (2)0.353 (3)3.364 (4)2.406
(5)0.942 (6)0.681 (7)1.687 (8)1.953
(9)0.720 (10)0.475 (11)1.698 (12)0.899
(13)0.971 (14)1.372 (15)0.584 (16)1.350
(17)0.960 (18)2.224 (19)2.926 (20)0.782
(21)1.079 (22)1.566 (23)0.880 (24)2.119
(25)0.169 (26)1.014 (27)0.804 (28)0.283
(29)3.381 (30)0.586 (31)0.728 (32)0.236

Page 76, Item 1:

(1)2.788 (2)0.845 (3)0.172 (4)3.091
(5)2.769 (6)0.344 (7)0.950 (8)0.051
(9)2.250 (10)1.941 (11)1.094 (12)0.200
(13)2.392 (14)1.086 (15)0.060 (16)1.868
(17)3.445 (18)2.311 (19)0.318 (20)0.707
(21)1.511 (22)2.644 (23)0.200 (24)1.413
(25)0.310 (26)2.409 (27)0.724 (28)2.210
(29)0.884 (30)1.238 (31)1.523 (32)1.097

Page 77, Item 1:

(1)1.379 (2)3.709 (3)1.885 (4)0.576
(5)1.850 (6)2.121 (7)2.358 (8)2.327
(9)0.432 (10)1.604 (11)0.783 (12)2.482
(13)2.796 (14)3.760 (15)2.554 (16)0.053
(17)3.244 (18)3.556 (19)2.077 (20)2.879
(21)0.215 (22)0.498 (23)0.885 (24)0.132
(25)1.275 (26)1.223 (27)0.099 (28)2.733
(29)1.295 (30)1.340 (31)1.787 (32)0.941

Page 78, Item 1:

(1)0.253 (2)2.020 (3)2.565 (4)3.694
(5)0.176 (6)3.131 (7)2.444 (8)0.079
(9)1.733 (10)0.138 (11)1.418 (12)0.339
(13)0.309 (14)2.300 (15)1.735 (16)0.534
(17)3.299 (18)0.263 (19)3.694 (20)1.556
(21)2.366 (22)2.530 (23)3.181 (24)1.497
(25)2.952 (26)1.198 (27)1.397 (28)1.477
(29)2.433 (30)0.860 (31)2.561 (32)2.182

Page 79, Item 1:

(1)2.280 (2)1.899 (3)3.457 (4)0.326
(5)1.667 (6)1.459 (7)1.033 (8)3.199
(9)1.746 (10)1.970 (11)0.025 (12)2.764
(13)1.568 (14)1.567 (15)1.282 (16)0.987

(17)3.042 (18)2.874 (19)0.735 (20)0.582
(21)0.137 (22)2.761 (23)2.029 (24)3.830
(25)3.090 (26)0.190 (27)3.443 (28)1.070
(29)2.711 (30)1.840 (31)2.542 (32)0.378

Page 81, Item 1:

(1)0.12 (2)12.48 (3)6.4 (4)1.92 (5)3.5
(6)0.76 (7)0.54 (8)4.07 (9)11.1 (10)1.35
(11)1.84 (12)8.75 (13)7.83 (14)0.28
(15)1.05 (16)4.6 (17)14.4 (18)0.36 (19)5.46
(20)7.98 (21)2.1 (22)0.03 (23)12.3 (24)6.2
(25)6.44 (26)0.9 (27)4.73 (28)1.7 (29)1.35
(30)0.63 (31)11.78 (32)8.06 (33)1.44
(34)0.6 (35)11.89 (36)5.75 (37)1.98
(38)1.32 (39)2.07 (40)0.63

Page 82, Item 1:

(1)12.58 (2)1.28 (3)9.68 (4)8.75 (5)9.99
(6)10.56 (7)1.96 (8)7.2 (9)3.74 (10)3.38
(11)7 (12)15.12 (13)6.45 (14)7.2 (15)3.22
(16)10.85 (17)5.18 (18)6.6 (19)2.86
(20)11.55 (21)15.2 (22)4.07 (23)0.68
(24)3.5 (25)1.55 (26)13.64 (27)2.25
(28)2.88 (29)1.8 (30)12.95 (31)9.25 (32)8.5
(33)7.56 (34)0.9 (35)1.61 (36)13.34 (37)2.2
(38)1.92 (39)0.37 (40)1.3

Page 83, Item 1:

(1)1.1 (2)2.16 (3)10.88 (4)1.6 (5)6.48
(6)9.31 (7)13.2 (8)2.34 (9)9.43 (10)14.04
(11)3.57 (12)15.17 (13)0.56 (14)1.47
(15)0.58 (16)0.6 (17)1.7 (18)11.96 (19)2.86
(20)18.13 (21)1.4 (22)7.28 (23)0.36
(24)0.42 (25)1.6 (26)1.74 (27)1.56 (28)8.05
(29)0.96

(30)1.19 (31)6.27 (32)9.9 (33)7.04 (34)4.6
(35)9.8 (36)3.77 (37)10.56 (38)8.64
(39)0.48 (40)0.76

Page 84, Item 1:
(1)3.2 (2)5.4 (3)17.5 (4)6.5 (5)4.32 (6)0.49
(7)4.03 (8)1.92 (9)7.2 (10)3.4 (11)4.94
(12)4.2 (13)3.44 (14)5.6 (15)9.31 (16)9.9
(17)6.38 (18)5.85 (19)8.7 (20)1.26 (21)4.48
(22)9.24 (23)0.15 (24)3.4 (25)3.52
(26)10.36 (27)6.4 (28)12.76 (29)5.78
(30)1.05 (31)0.6 (32)16.92 (33)1.82
(34)0.03 (35)8.88 (36)0.84 (37)1.7 (38)2.04
(39)6.84 (40)6.24

Page 85, Item 1:
(1)1.24 (2)8.64 (3)15.12 (4)6.4 (5)6.27
(6)3.19 (7)4.2 (8)5.25 (9)7.48 (10)0.42
(11)6.84 (12)6.65 (13)1.76 (14)1.24
(15)13.6 (16)10 (17)12.69 (18)2.04 (19)7.26
(20)2.28 (21)5.12 (22)6.96 (23)11.31
(24)9.24 (25)2.34 (26)1.08 (27)9.68
(28)0.68 (29)0.06 (30)4.8 (31)1.35 (32)6.84
(33)8 (34)1.53 (35)8.36 (36)1.48 (37)3.68
(38)7.13 (39)0.72 (40)2.76

Page 86, Item 1:
(1)2.64 (2)0.48 (3)1.89 (4)0.05 (5)0.35
(6)3.48 (7)17.16 (8)7.75 (9)2.24 (10)14.04
(11)7.84 (12)6.46 (13)4.25 (14)11.2
(15)5.46 (16)7.48 (17)0.26 (18)4.84 (19)1.7
(20)2.32 (21)4.8 (22)9 (23)2.66 (24)7.04
(25)3.99 (26)5.58 (27)2 (28)0.39 (29)0.95
(30)7.52 (31)4.41 (32)6 (33)2 (34)5.12
(35)2.52 (36)1.92 (37)6.27 (38)0.65
(39)5.33 (40)0.72

Page 88, Item 1:
(1)8.2 (2)0.7 (3)1.6 (4)0.2 (5)2 (6)29 (7)5
(8)1 (9)0.1 (10)0.5 (11)1.9 (12)2.1 (13)1
(14)0.1 (15)1.5 (16)0.4 (17)1.5 (18)1 (19)8
(20)0.6 (21)0.2 (22)1.5 (23)1.7 (24)1.2
(25)1.2 (26)2.1 (27)1.9 (28)0.5 (29)0.2
(30)0.4 (31)6.5 (32)0.4 (33)3.1 (34)0.6

(35)1.4 (36)1.5 (37)4.4 (38)1.9 (39)8 (40)0.8

Page 89, Item 1:
(1)1.6 (2)1.2 (3)1.1 (4)2.6 (5)0.4 (6)1.5
(7)0.7 (8)1.6 (9)1 (10)4.4 (11)1.8 (12)2.2
(13)0.8 (14)1.3 (15)1.5 (16)10.5 (17)1
(18)0.8 (19)0.1 (20)2.8 (21)0.7 (22)3.9
(23)6.1 (24)1 (25)6 (26)40 (27)0.7 (28)0.3
(29)15 (30)Infinity (31)10 (32)2.4 (33)1.8
(34)1.8 (35)9.8 (36)1.3 (37)1.4 (38)2 (39)4.6
(40)1.7

Page 90, Item 1:
(1)5.1 (2)0.7 (3)0.6 (4)0.4 (5)0.4 (6)0.1
(7)0.9 (8)0.9 (9)0.9 (10)7.2 (11)11.8 (12)0.2
(13)0.3 (14)0.5 (15)1.6 (16)0.2 (17)0.5
(18)Infinity (19)1.2 (20)0.3 (21)0.4 (22)1.3
(23)8 (24)0.4 (25)0.8 (26)1.2 (27)0.5 (28)1.4
(29)2.9 (30)2.5 (31)5.1 (32)1.9 (33)17.5
(34)1.7 (35)2.3 (36)0.3 (37)0.4 (38)1.3
(39)0.4 (40)2.6

Page 91, Item 1:
(1)0.8 (2)0.7 (3)3 (4)1.6 (5)5.3 (6)0.9 (7)3.3
(8)12 (9)1.7 (10)2.9 (11)0.5 (12)1
(13)Infinity (14)8 (15)1.4 (16)2.2 (17)2.4
(18)3.9 (19)1.5 (20)0.6 (21)1.1 (22)1.2
(23)2.5 (24)0.9 (25)3.3 (26)1.5 (27)1.2
(28)1.2 (29)0.9 (30)1.9 (31)0.9 (32)1.4
(33)3.6 (34)2.1 (35)1.3 (36)1.1 (37)0.1
(38)0.5 (39)3.5 (40)1

Page 92, Item 1:
(1)0.2 (2)0.6 (3)2.8 (4)2.2 (5)0.5 (6)0.9
(7)1.4 (8)1.3 (9)2.5 (10)7 (11)0.2 (12)0.8
(13)1.1 (14)0.1 (15)0.7 (16)2 (17)0.4 (18)0.8
(19)0.2 (20)1.7 (21)6.3 (22)2.8 (23)1 (24)1.5

(25)1.2 (26)1.1 (27)1.1 (28)1.1 (29)2 (30)2.1
(31)1.5 (32)1.5 (33)3 (34)0.7 (35)2.6 (36)1
(37)38 (38)9.8 (39)0.5 (40)1.4
Page 93, Item 1:
(1)3.9 (2)0.9 (3)2.1 (4)2 (5)0.6 (6)0.5 (7)3.8
(8)0.1 (9)0.1 (10)1.8 (11)0.2 (12)3.2 (13)0.7
(14)9.3 (15)21 (16)1.2 (17)1.2 (18)2.1
(19)1.1 (20)0.8 (21)0.3 (22)0.9 (23)1.2 (24)4
(25)0.7 (26)0.7 (27)18.5 (28)2.2 (29)1.2
(30)1.7 (31)0.4 (32)0.7 (33)3.1 (34)0.5
(35)1.8 (36)0.5 (37)0.8 (38)0.6 (39)0.4
(40)1.3

Made in the USA
Las Vegas, NV
25 August 2024

94412993R00063